A PLUME BOOK

THIS OLD SPOUSE

SHARYN WOLF, CSW, is a Manhattan-based therapist (and home-owner), specializing in long-married couples. She has led relationship and dating workshops in cities from Boston to Seattle, and in 2005, she served as a national spokesperson and consultant for Viagra. A regular media presence and commentator on celebrity marriages and modern romance, Sharyn has been a frequent guest on dozens of TV and radio shows, including *Oprah*, *48 Hours*, and CNN. Her work has been profiled internationally in publications such as *Newsweek*, the *Boston Globe*, the *Washington Post*, the *Seattle Times*, and the *New York Times*.

This Old Spouse

Tips and Tools for Keeping the Honeymoon Glow

Sharyn Wolf

21956L

A PLUME BOOK

PLUME
Published by the Penguin Group
Penguin Group (USA) Inc., 375 Hudson Street, New York, New York 10014, U.S.A. •
Penguin Group (Canada), 90 Eglinton Avenue East, Suite 700, Toronto, Ontario, Canada
M4P 2Y3 (a division of Pearson Penguin Canada Inc.) • Penguin Books Ltd., 80 Strand, London
WC2R 0RL, England • Penguin Ireland, 25 St. Stephen's Green, Dublin 2, Ireland (a division
of Penguin Books Ltd.) • Penguin Group (Australia), 250 Camberwell Road, Camberwell,
Victoria 3124, Australia (a division of Pearson Australia Group Pty. Ltd.) • Penguin Books
India Pvt. Ltd., 11 Community Centre, Panchsheel Park, New Delhi – 110 017, India •
Penguin Group (NZ), 67 Apollo Drive, Rosedale, North Shore 0632, New Zealand (a division
of Pearson New Zealand Ltd.) • Penguin Books (South Africa) (Pty.) Ltd., 24 Sturdee Avenue,
Rosebank, Johannesburg 2196, South Africa

Penguin Books Ltd., Registered Offices: 80 Strand, London WC2R 0RL, England

Published by Plume, a member of Penguin Group (USA) Inc. Previously published in a
Hudson Street Press edition.

First Plume Printing, July 2008
10 9 8 7 6 5 4 3 2 1

 REGISTERED TRADEMARK—MARCA REGISTRADA

The Library of Congress has catalogued the Hudson Street Press edition as follows:

Wolf, Sharyn
   This old spouse : a unique do-it-yourself guide to restoring, renovating, and rebuilding your
relationship / Sharyn Wolf.
      p.   cm.
   ISBN 978-1-59463-036-1 (hc.)
   ISBN 978-0-452-28951-2 (pbk.)
1.   Marriage.   2.   Man-woman relationships.   1.   Title.
   HQ734. W852 2007
   646.7'8--dc22   2007008002

Printed in the United States of America

For Betsy Carpenter

Contents

PART 3. Major Repairs

PART 4. Spouse Proud

Being deeply loved by someone gives you strength—
being someone who loves deeply gives you courage.
—LaoTzu

I thought I loved you, Ossie, when we got married,
but as I see it now, I was only in the kindergarten of
the proposition. To arrive at love is like working on
a double doctorate in the subject of life.
—Ruby Dee

PART 1

Evaluating, Appraising, and Inspecting Your Marriage

CHAPTER 1

How Falling in Love with a Spouse Is Like Falling in Love with a House, for Better and Worse

Remember when you were single? Those frustrating weekends when you weren't sure you'd *ever* find someone to settle down with? Those nights when you began to doubt that there was anyone in your species, let alone your age range, to whom you could picture yourself saying "I do"?

And then it happened. He appeared. And even if he wasn't exactly who you'd had in mind, before long you realized how perfect he was for you. Your heart beat fast enough. He made you laugh enough. He wanted enough of what you wanted. You not only loved him, you loved how you felt about yourself when you were with him. Before you knew it, you were married.

Even if, looking back at your single years, it seemed like a hop, skip, and jump down the aisle—and even if you knew after your very first date with your husband that you were meant to be together— your transformation from an ambivalent singleton to a "ready-to-wed" bride probably didn't happen suddenly. More likely, it happened step by step, goal by goal, late night talk by late night talk.

Becoming a homeowner is a similar process. Many twenty- or thirtysomethings postpone buying a home, not because they particularly enjoy being told they can't paint or hang anything on the walls, but because they equate it with the burden and the responsibilities of home ownership: mortgages, utility bills, lawns, and no super in sight.

As men and women mature, however, their desires mature with them. What renters don't remember the shock of the first time they calculated how much money they'd paid in rent over the years with nothing to show for it? How many cannot recall the annoyance they felt when they were told they absolutely could not have shelves installed in the living room, let alone take in little Millie, the stray cat they'd been feeding regularly? Eventually, the idea of owning their own home moves from being merely appealing to seeming quite necessary.

This is when potential home-buyers, who usually don't yet have nearly enough money for a down payment, grab that pencil and begin their first serious circling in the Real Estate section, dreaming about the kind of home they might one day call their own.

This is a crucial stage, because, as anyone who has been through it can attest, house-hunters have to trudge through a lot of homes before they finally float through the one that they both can actually afford (if they give up mochaccinos, movies, and new furniture for life), and want to live in—the house that is not only available but that they genuinely love.

The search can last months, even years. A house-hunter can reject home after home that others would be perfectly happy with, for no other reason than the house doesn't feel right. Something intangible is missing. She just can't see herself cooking lasagna in that kitchen or watching her favorite TV shows in that living room or setting up a swing set in that backyard. She can't really explain it to the real estate agent. She only knows she has to keep looking.

And then, maybe on the day she was about to give up, it happens. She walks up another path through another door into another house, and this time she hears the Hallelujah chorus. So what if the house needs work? She's already envisioning the dinner parties she'll throw in its high-ceilinged dining room. She has already fallen in love with the wide-plank floors, the swirling banister leading to the upstairs bedrooms, and the claw-footed tub in the master bath. It's not as if she ignores the yellowing wallpaper or the clunky radiators, or the small, dark living room. She'll take down a wall and open it up. And a good paint job will do wonders. Everything else can be fixed. Somehow, it will all work out. The charm of the house is overpowering. She walks out on the back porch and sees an overgrown vegetable garden in the yard. By spring she could be standing in the same spot with a cup of coffee in one hand and a few tulip bulbs in the other. Not that she's ever planted anything before. Not that, when you come to think of it, she's even been able to keep a houseplant alive. Still, her excitement is like a drug. This is it. This is home.

Love often works the same way. A woman can date a decent crop of eligible suitors with superior résumés (not to mention the losers she should have taken a crop to) and feel nothing—not a single hormonal ping. Her friends may tell her she's too picky, that she'll end up alone. She may even start to believe them. And then one day she trips over a lanky stranger at a Super Bowl party or snickers about the airline food to the man seated next to her, and the hormones go into overdrive—unexpected, tingly, and delicious. The two of them start dating and before long they're inseparable.

They meet each other's friends and find them charming or, at least, tolerable. They meet each other's families and everyone survives. Then one night he comes down with the flu and she goes over to his apartment with chicken soup. He opens the door bleary-eyed, honking his nose and wearing mismatched socks, and she is sure he has never looked more adorable. And so it goes. For better or worse (or, better *and* worse), he's the one.

And, that's where our story—for couples and home-buyers—begins.

How Getting to Know a Spouse Is Like Getting to Know a House

Remember our home-buyer who was sure she'd found her dream house? Today she's unpacking a mountain of boxes in her new home. It's spring. The sun is setting, and she takes a short break. Sitting on the living room floor eating moo shu chicken out of a carton, she can't help but notice that even the food tastes better here. She's exhausted and happy and sure she made the right decision.

Spring turns to summer. With her friends on the patio for a dinner party, she returns to the kitchen to refill the pitcher of sangria and notices flies buzzing around the guacamole. Did she leave a window screen up? No, they're all down, but on closer inspection she sees that one screen doesn't fit properly because the window frame is warped. Hmmm. She's hoping it can be fixed without too much trouble.

By July, she discovers that the two upstairs bedrooms aren't well ventilated. She hopes the new fans will do the trick, but they don't, and she eventually gives in and buys air conditioners—an expense she hadn't anticipated. After she and a friend wrestle them into the window, jerry-rigging cardboard and foam to fill in the sides (doesn't that look nice?), she turns one on and the power goes out.

Replacing the fuses doesn't solve the problem. She calls an electrician who says he'll be there first thing Monday morning but doesn't show up until well past noon, causing her to miss a meeting at her office. With the power back on he tells her everything should be fine as long as she doesn't run more than one air conditioner at a time. "But the inspector said the wiring was fine," she whines. "It's fine on the first floor," he tells her. Inquiring further, she discovers that the wiring on the second floor was installed during the Roosevelt administration.

Teddy.

Next to go? That beautiful claw-footed tub in the master bath suddenly refuses to drain. Unable to unclog it herself, she calls another $100-an-hour professional who arrives, snake in hand, and leaves with another oversized check.

Overwhelmed, and feeling a little nauseous, she collapses on her living room couch, not knowing whether to laugh or cry. "What have I gotten myself into?" she moans. "This may have been one helluva mistake."

That first scent encountered on the trail of serious doubts and second thoughts comes to just about all home-buyers, eventually. And sooner or later, it comes to just about all wives and husbands, too.

It's inevitable. Human beings, like houses, are full of quirks and secrets that aren't revealed on first or even subsequent visits. A woman can date a man for years, she can know his deepest fears, she can spend a week on a cruise alone with his mother, she can even move in with him (or he with her), and she will still be in for unexpected jolts after they get married.

There's no possible way for someone to know all the flaws of a house—that mice rule the basement or that the attic roof leaks when it rains—until he or she has signed the deed, moved in, and taken up permanent residence. The same is true in marriage. There's no way for a woman to know that her husband will always have issues with his boss, no matter where he works, until after they've been married for a certain length of time. Moreover, it can take years to learn that all those times he was nodding his head in assent—which she interpreted as *listening*—he was really just trying to stay awake while she talked.

And so it is that women and men fall in love with a partner in much the same way that they fall in love with a house: in both cases, with a few stars in their eyes. They know, or think they know, that marriage, like home ownership, will take work, but they never really guessed how much. They prefer to believe that they can handle whatever challenges come their way. If they didn't, they'd all still be renting.

This honeymoon-like state of mind generally makes the first few months or even the first few years blissful. We almost forget that people who love each other can still hurt each other, and that small hurts and disappointments pile up. We manage to brush them aside until, one day, the flaws that a new wife or homeowner thought would never matter start to matter—*really* matter. Whatever she missed or chose to overlook suddenly insinuates itself into her consciousness, making her chronically short-tempered and tired. What she thought was a charming old porch turns out to have gross rot. What she saw as her husband's sense of spontaneity turns out to be a troubling lack of impulse control. The day always comes when the new wife—similar to our new homeowner above—takes off the rose-colored glasses and starts muttering, "If only I had known."

And then: "Did I make a mistake?"

Thankfully, the answer is, almost always, *no*. All spouses and all homeowners experience ups and downs. It's just that at some point there will be a lot of downs, all happening at the same time. Some people quit at this stage and start looking for an easier relationship with fewer flaws—a different house or another spouse. But no matter what television show you watch or what romantic saga you read, there are no easy relationships between spouses! *When it comes to marriage, they're all fixer-uppers*.

If you have reached this stage in your own marriage, the one where the honeymoon period you didn't realize was a honeymoon period is over, then you are likely to be feeling bombarded by the problems and deficiencies in your marriage and partner (because, of course, it's all his fault—anyone can see that!) as you have never felt bombarded before. Can you ever really be happy enough with this guy now that you understand who he really is, how he really operates, and how much work it will take?

The answer is *yes*, and I'm here to help you do it.

Who I Am and What I Know

During almost twenty years of practice as a marriage counselor in New York City, I have worked with couples in every stage of relationships, from couples who've just started living together to couples well into the double-digit years of marriage. I've counseled couples with no children, young children, older children, children out of the nest, and children whom couples wish would leave the nest. I've worked with partners and families of every configuration you can imagine and a few you probably can't. I've worked with

partners who complained of boredom or emotional fatigue and
partners who were fighting about children, stepchildren, in-laws,
money, or sex—all of the usual and some of the extraordinary. I've
sat with couples who swear they hate each other and then leave my
office and go get an ice cream cone together. From the wife who lost
her temper because her husband refused to wash and recycle plastic
toothpicks to the husband who took his wife on a fifty-mile bike
ride her first time on a bike since junior high (akin to a kind of
lower extremities torture), I've pretty much heard it all.

I always start where the couple wants to start—trying to work
through the problem that brought them to my office. For example, if
every time Lionel and Helen have a bad argument he storms out and
leaves her feeling angry and abandoned, it's manageable to ask him
to agree that the next time he's heading out the door he will clearly
say to her, "Helen, I'm leaving and I'll be back in an hour when I cool
down." I don't immediately try to get them to stop fighting or tell
Lionel he shouldn't leave. Because Lionel actually may be avoiding
an even bigger fight. It's not the leaving that is the problem. It is letting Helen think he is unwilling to work at it with her. As long as she
knows he isn't dropping the issue, Lionel and Helen will do fine.

Once both partners get the initial problem under control, I try next
to direct them toward an examination and evaluation of the way they
argue or the way they tackle their problems. Why? Because, as with
Lionel's walking out, this is almost always a greater source of conflict
than the problem itself. Discovering new ways to talk about problems
leads to feeling safer in the relationship. Expressing curiosity and
respect for each other's feelings by saying something like "I'm not
sure I understand what you're saying—could you pass that by me
again?" always produces a better outcome than yelling, "How could
you do this to me?" or "When will you try to make some sense?"

When couples approach problems the wrong way, even with the right intentions, they usually end up making things worse.

Finally, I strongly believe what you may already know: that a good laugh between spouses provides more healing than a thousand explanations of what he or she meant to say. Laughing at yourself, a little good-natured poking fun at your partner, a recognition of the humor of life's absurdities: When you and your partner laugh together, you are building up your bank account of goodwill.

This is my fifth book. In three previous books on dating, *50 Ways to Find a Lover*, *Guerrilla Dating Tactics*, and *So You Want to Get Married*, I offered practical advice to single women and men about what might be getting in the way of their finding the serious love relationship they so dearly wanted but could not seem to locate. In my fourth book and first on marriage, *How to Stay Lovers for Life*, I drew from my years of training and practice to help newlywed couples anticipate and manage the predictable challenges of early married life.

Shortly after my fourth book was published, I became a first-time homeowner myself. I hadn't been planning to buy anything in the ever costly New York City. So I was stunned when a friend called me and took me to a first-floor apartment that she warned me was a real fixer-upper in Greenwich Village, and I fell in love with it at first sight. Blinded by the possibilities—the basement was also available and could be converted into an office space for my practice—and high on an optimistic faith in my ability to handle the work required, I was sure that this was the home I was meant to own. And so, without much preparation or trepidation, I took the plunge, never really understanding how deep the drop would be.

Like every home purchase, it was a huge investment. And like every fixer-upper, it ended up being a lot more fixer than upper. Soon enough, after the basement flooded twice, after the boiler broke down and they had to break down my door to take the boiler out, after the water in the shower went from warm to scalding (with me in it), I began to get a gnawing sense that behind every $200 repair a $2,000 repair lurked, waiting to mess with me. At one point near the end of the renovation, when the builders stopped showing up and the mess remained untouched for weeks, with a thick coat of Sheetrock dust covering everything, I sat down in the middle of the living room floor and started to cry.

And that's when it hit me: This was a lot like love.

The same idyllic beginning, the same serious commitment, the same goofy honeymoon period, the same eventual Bismarck feeling that I was sinking fast, the same worries about whether I had made the right decision.

I tried to pull myself out of it by being my own couple counselor. I tried everything in my psychotherapy tool kit to calm myself down. I told myself not to catastrophize by lumping everything together into one overwhelming drama. I reminded myself that the house was not collapsing and the roof was not crashing down— even if it felt that way. I reassured myself that I didn't have to try to fix everything at once. I reached out to others who would remind me of how far I'd come. I learned to be happy with small successes.

Let's Talk About Plumbing and Heating

I also started thinking that maybe I was on to something—that maybe I could put a bad experience to good use. What if this was a fresh idea for couple counseling?

And so, the next week, when Fred turned away from Kate, saying that he thought they were beyond help, I began talking about tools for renovation and relationship repair. I brought up the subject of the plumbing and heating, strengthening foundations and tearing down walls. Fred perked up and said, "Plumbing? Tell me what you know about unclogging pipes." It felt playful and natural as long as I didn't overdo it, and I hadn't heard Fred make a joke in an awfully long time. I soon found that other men took to talking about their marriage in terms of plumbing and hammers and cement as well. The silliness and non-blaming familiarity of these terms gave them license to talk about feelings and other intimate matters without experiencing too much emotional discomfort or feeling overexposed. A phrase such as "Let's talk about plumbing and heating" brought a much better response than "How's your sex life these days?"

Women liked it because it inspired men to talk more, and because these metaphors reduced their emotional distress. "We have a wall between us" seemed less harsh or irreversible than "He refuses to talk about anything important." A wall can come down, and framing the problem that way helped many wives to see conflicts as temporary hurdles rather than as permanent and hopeless. I also started applying household terms to some common couple interactions, such as what I call the "junk drawer" fight—the conflict in which partners pull out their messy assortment of every resentment that's not nailed down and hurl them at each other. Just giving these fights a silly label helped couples feel less guilty about having them, and more willing to discuss them.

The most useful part of applying the language of home repair to marital problems was that it helped partners grasp that relationships are not good or bad, right or wrong, black or white, perfect or hopeless, but more of an ongoing project—a process of improvement, setback, upgrade, maintenance, reassessment, and repair, very much like the never-ending process of maintaining and improving a home. It helped them see that, like maintaining and improving a home, the work of maintaining and improving a relationship is never finished.

This leads us to the questions that form the core of this book: Can couples find deep happiness in a marriage and take deep pride in the improvements they've made in it, even though the relationship isn't and will never be perfect? My experience as a homeowner and as a marriage counselor tells me that the answer is *yes*.

In the decade since I published my previous book and bought my home, I have gained an even deeper understanding of why some marriages thrive while other marriages flounder. Not long ago, I began to feel an eagerness to share what I've learned during the past ten years in a new book, but I wondered how to present that material in a fresh, practical, easy-to-follow, and playful manner. (Relationships are hard enough. Who needs a relationship book that feels like work?) As I sat in the living room considering the possibilities, my thoughts wandered back to that moment ten years earlier when I lay crying on the floor of the same room, and I suddenly grasped the parallels between home ownership and love—and in that moment, the structure of this book became clear.

The Only Do-It-Yourself Marriage Repair Guide You'll Ever Need

The purpose of this book is to teach you to act as your own "marriage contractor." In the sections and chapters that follow, I will walk you through the process of renovating, restoring, and making repairs in your marriage in much the same way a contractor might assess and propose repairs and make improvements to your home.

In Part 1: Evaluating, Appraising, and Inspecting Your Marriage, you will learn how to calmly and accurately reappraise the value of your spouse and marriage (you're almost sure to find they're far more valuable than you think), and how to do a quick, preliminary check for basic structural integrity or damage.

In Part 2: Planning and Prep Work, you will learn how to envision the marriage you want and draw up plans for building it; which tools, skills, and supplies you need to have on hand and (just as important) which to toss out before you start making improvements.

In Part 3: Major Repairs, you will learn how to make basic, essential repairs to three key aspects of your marriage: the heating system (your sex life); the wiring (communication); and your intimacy and connectedness.

And in Part 4: Spouse Proud, I'll help you add finishing touches to your marriage renovation; provide problem-averting marriage maintenance techniques; guide you in deciding when to stop making improvements and move on to another project (and what that project might be); and offer thoughts on how to celebrate your accomplishments.

Fair warning, though. Repairing, restoring, or renovating a relationship takes at least as much time and care and commitment as refinishing an antique dresser. If you truly want to restore the original beauty, be prepared to learn the real meaning of "a labor of love."

Repairs also need to be done properly if they are to withstand the test of time. Painting over a crack in the bathroom ceiling doesn't fix the crack. In fact, over time, that crack will become bigger and bigger until, one day, you'll come home from the supermarket to find half your bathroom ceiling lying in the tub. Trust me—putting in the work *now*, while the crack is still just a crack, will help to prevent calamities down the road.

In addition, you will likely face repairs in places that have no visible damage now. (Inadequate wiring does not manifest itself until you accidentally overload it.) This book will help you assess what's going on beneath the surface in your marriage, in those places you can't quite see, so that if any repairs or upgrades do need to be made, you can tackle them smartly.

The good news, and there is a lot of it, is that not all repairs (to a relationship or a home) are major undertakings. This book will offer quick fixes and simple patches that can do wonders for the look of the living room or the look of love. Plus, if you have ever thrown your hands in the air and said, "Why is this happening to me? What did I do wrong?" this book will point you toward those places where you add to the wear and tear on your marriage—inadvertently, of course—and offer answers.

Remember, you can't tackle everything you might want to improve in your relationship or house all at once. Knowing where to start and what to wait on will save you more than a few gray hairs. We'll hit the hot spots, but we'll pace ourselves.

Here are some other ground rules to keep in mind.

• *Wear your hard hat.* Accidents happen during relationship repairs and renovations just as they do during home repair projects. Truths sometimes get spoken that need to be spoken, but a husband or wife may not want to hear them. Feelings can get injured, and even minor injuries hurt. Band-Aids and other first-aid equipment will be provided in the pages that follow.

• *Be prepared to live with the mess.* Things will likely get messy and possibly worse before they get better. Tearing down walls in a house or relationship creates dust and debris. When the mess seems overwhelming, stick your head out the window and yell, "This, too, shall pass!"

* *Expect the job to go over schedule.* Sometimes what looks like a simple home repair turns out not to be. A home-buyer removes a broken wall tile in the bathroom and discovers a major hole in the supporting wall. And sometimes a minor marriage problem isn't so minor. Many couples fall into the habit of minimizing problems to avoid conflict. Help will be there if you discover that the anger and disappointments go deeper than you thought.

* *Don't seek too many outside opinions.* Experienced do-it-yourselfers often consult experts before tackling a project for the first time, but they do so selectively, knowing that every expert will have a different opinion and that some of the advice will be wrong for them. Couples need to be just as choosy about discussing marital issues with outsiders. They need to be aware that even close friends and relatives can give lousy advice and may not have the couple's best interests at heart, even when they think they do. On days when you feel like you've had it with your husband and need a compassionate ear to vent to, look for a trusted person who understands the challenges of a long-term relationship and who won't encourage you to quit only because the going has gotten a little rough.

* *Take scheduled breaks.* Repairs that require careful concentration for long stretches of time can be exhausting, and working past the point of exhaustion can lead to accidents. I advise couples I'm counseling to allow sufficient breaks from working on their relationship by scheduling time for fun, relaxation, and rest: getting more sleep; taking long walks; going to movies; doing yoga—*not*

talking about "the relationship." I also advise them to rehearse a relationship "fire drill," knowing where they'll go, what they'll do,
who'll they'll visit when they are too exhausted to keep working
(and perhaps need a break from each other).

• *Keep your eye on the goal.* Do-it-yourselfers will have good days,
when they feel like they're making great progress, and they will
have bad days, when they feel like they're losing ground. This is
when homeowners pull out the sketch of what the new kitchen,
bathroom, or deck will look like when it's finished and remind
themselves what they're working toward. This is when couples
need to do the same thing. The fact that you're reading this book
suggests that you and your husband still love each other even
though you may not have been great at expressing it lately. So, if
you've been bickering for a while now without really knowing what
you're fighting about, now you know. You're fighting for your
marriage.

• *Do whatever it takes.* Okay. You bought the book. This tells us
that, for the moment, you are the more motivated partner. Even if
you frequently fall into that role, it's possible that the only way to get
an improvement project going this time is if you kick it off—again.
However, I bet you've got a husband who will be grateful if you do,
because he cares as much about the marriage as you do. In my practice, I've heard many wives complain, "Why does it always have to
be me?" and I empathize. But if the outcome can be a happier, more
satisfying marriage, does it really matter who goes first? More to the
point: If you *don't* go first, and for whatever reason your husband
can't, who will?

The bottom line is that this is *your* life and marriage, and he is *your* old spouse. No one knows better than you do what needs doing, tending, repairing, or fixing to live happily ever after together. No one is better qualified to initiate and supervise the job. All you need is some help and guidance.

That's where I come in. I'm here to show you how.

CHAPTER 2

When's the Last Time You Had Your Spouse Appraised?

Don't Underestimate the Value of What You Have!

Y ou now know the many ways in which falling in love with a spouse is like falling in love with a house—the early stage when people are bowled over by a combination of what they see and what they want/yearn/need to see. Any way you look at it, when love strikes, realistic evaluation is slow to follow. One day, though, those fingernail clippings in the bed will appear to be exactly what they are: gross! The phone call he promised to make and didn't make will be seen for exactly what it is: rude! And so, we wake up on the fairy tale's flip side—in the dark pond where the prince reverts to being a toad, if he ever was a prince at all.

This realization has to happen, but take heart. Just as the honeymoon stage passes, the phase where your partner seems to have been replaced by his evil twin passes, too. In fact, both marriage and housing share the same four stages of romance.

The Four Stages of Romantic Love

Stage One: Idealization. The first is the idealization stage, when you finally discover the man or the home of your dreams. During this stage, we dwell on the perfection of our beloved man or home. Fate has been kind to us. We've found the most wonderful place to live or the most wonderful partner a woman could want. At the time, the love and adoration we experience feels like it will last forever.

Stage Two: The Disappointment Phase. Then, as I described in the last chapter, the banister cracks or your spouse hasn't picked up his stuff since the Clinton administration. A wife thinks, "If only I could fix the banister and it would stay fixed" or "If only he remembered that dirty socks are not carpet accessories, everything will be fine." "If only this/if only that" is another way of saying that she's disappointed, but she believes that by making just a few small changes in her house or husband, her brewing disappointments will ease, and she can go back to idealization.

Stage Three: The Devaluation Stage. But things don't stay fixed and her husband doesn't listen to the way she wants him to live his life. Now, after what seems an eternity of little things breaking down in house and heart, she decides that it is not the banister or the socks that are the problems. It is the house or the spouse that is seriously flawed—and that's permanent. Thoughts move from "If only he would go back to the way he was and treat me the way he used to, I'd be happy" to "This house is a lemon" and "This spouse is a turkey." Both home and husband are summarily devalued at their very core; the house and the mate are simply not good enough. I'll come back to this later, but for now, please understand that these are only stages in time—stages that almost all couples go through—not life sentences.

Stage Four: The Pride and Appreciation Stage. Devaluation may seem like a terrible place to end up after that huge investment of money or love. However, it's actually quite a good place to find yourself, because soon, instead of living off of hormonal fancies with Cupid's arrow stuck in your heart (or loins), you get the chance to construct a strong marriage based on a solid exchange of respect, work, caring, work, affection—and work. Homeowners and couples who do that work eventually reach the fourth stage, experiencing pride and appreciation when their house or spouse doesn't seem like a jewel that was bestowed upon them, but rather a jewel they mined and polished themselves. It feels more tangible—and valuable. This good relationship can withstand trouble. Plus it can't be destroyed when a dishwasher breaks or an errant sock shows up because now spouses know what to do about such things.

When devaluation hits, couples go in one of two directions: They either bail and move on to another person with whom they will repeat these same three stages (even if they don't know that now), or they stay and do what needs to be done to reach Stage Four and turn a devalued relationship into a solid, lasting love.

Some women, when they reach the devaluation stage, still choose to believe that it was fate that brought them together with house or husband and think, "If we're meant to be together, we'll stay together." If you fall into this group, I hope you will consider that fate is highly overrated and, most likely, you would never let it determine your work ethic or parenting style. You'd never say, "If I'm meant to get a promotion, I'll get one" or "If I'm meant to raise good kids, they'll be good." So why would you ever think you can turn over love to fate? It's a bad idea, any way you look at it.

The goal of this book is to get you past the devaluation phase and launch you well into the pride and appreciation stage. This chapter is going to talk about how it feels to be at Stage Three and what you have to do to force yourself out. I do not use the word "force" lightly. For a while, that may be what it takes.

How Much Are Man and Marriage Really Worth to You?

As less pleasant aspects of living in a particular house and with a particular spouse start to surface, you may experience an almost overwhelming, even scary sense of how many things need work and how much work things need. You didn't know that sound traveled through the house as if everyone were always in the same room together. You didn't know he assumed that his mother would move in when she got older. You didn't realize that the city's faulty sewer line would become the bane of your existence. You never dreamed he'd comment on the weight you gained while carrying *his* child. As your lives move forward together, things that were never issues become issues. Things once thought to be easy fixes aren't. You and your husband may find it harder and harder to contain yourselves when these problems that neither of you realized you were taking on just keep coming—in droves, it seems. Moreover, it becomes increasingly clear that, while certain issues can be resolved rather easily, others feel hopelessly insoluble.

If this scenario sounds like your marriage, welcome to the stage you thought would never come: the devaluation stage. With spouses and houses, there will almost always be a period when there is no middle ground. Homeowners and spouses do a 180-degree flip: Whereas they once were blind to the negatives, disappointment now blinds them to the positives. In this tricky and troubled stage of marriage, perceptions become deeply distorted, in a way opposite from the idealization stage. Now, instead of dreams and possibilities, there are nightmares and disillusionment. Flaws and a couple's reactions to them rule the day. Spouses lose sight of all the real beauty and sound value in their marriage. They lose sight of all the good reasons they decided to marry. In this disillusioned state, it often takes only one small additional problem—a gas tank a mate forgot to fill—to send them into despair. Nothing seems worth it.

Sometimes, when homeowners reach this point—they're really, really tired of the pipes freezing every winter or the squirrels getting into the attic every spring—they may start thinking about selling their current home and buying another one, a better one, a bigger or smaller, older or newer one with more or less property farther out from or closer to town. Anything but what they've got! Before putting a "For Sale" sign on the lawn, though, most homeowners will do a reality check and ask a professional appraiser or real estate broker to help them get an idea of the "fair market value" of their home. In other words, they want to know whether, if they sell now, they will lose or make money. If they sell later, will the value go up or down? This assessment may shock them—pleasantly or unpleasantly— when they discover the massive unknown worth of what they've got, not to mention the skyrocketing prices of the square boxes in a nearby zip code. They may wonder how they could have been so blind to what their house is really worth and how much other people would be willing to pay for it. They may also feel pretty pleased about how smart they were to have bought their house when they did, and to have done all the work they've put into it. They may shake their heads at how close they came to making a big, stupid mistake. Hell, they're not going to sell at all. They've picked a winner!

Sometimes, when a woman reaches a similar state of devaluation in her marriage—when she has grown really tired of the way her husband keeps running up his credit card bills or ogling other women in her presence or never letting her finish a sentence when they're out to dinner with friends—I'll encourage her to do a similar reappraisal of her marriage to help her get a clearer sense of the worth and value she can't see in her current distressed state.*

How about you? Do you think you could use an intelligent appraisal of your marriage like the one homeowners might have obtained for a house? If your marriage has reached the devaluation stage, I can assure you that a reappraisal is needed and can help you discover some things you're unable to see right now on your own. I can tell you that no matter where you think you are in your marriage right now, you might be very surprised by how good you've got it: how much more solid and valuable your relationship is than you think—and how much *more* solid and valuable it could become with a little more renovation and repair.

So let's get started.

---

* If you feel more than merely distressed, if you find yourself feeling enraged, depressed, and teary and it lasts for more than a few days, turn to the Appendix: FEMA for Relationships, at the back of the book. Help is there.

Twelve Easy Steps for Appraising
Your Relationship

1. Center yourself. Before you begin, go for a walk, get some fresh air, do whatever you need to do to calm yourself and quell those negative emotions you may be feeling at the moment about your husband. Remind yourself that whatever problems the two of you may be having, you both mean well. One of the cardinal tenets of home appraising is that appraisers, Realtors, and buyers don't really care how homeowners *feel* about a house they're selling, whether they love it or hate it, whether they can't bear the thought of selling or can't wait to leave. All they want to know about are the pluses and minuses, strong points and weak points, advantages and disadvantages. You want to strive for a similar objectivity when you evaluate your spouse and marriage.

If your usual methods of relaxing and calming yourself don't help lessen the negative feelings you're harboring, you may need to release them. This is not the time to spew them at your husband, though. (In Chapters 5 and 6, I'll help you sort through your communication toolbox to see how well equipped you are to share hurts and frustrations with your partner, and in Chapter 9, I'll help you develop new skills for discussing sensitive issues.) For now, instead of trying to express these feelings to your husband, it's better to spill them on paper instead.

Try this: Write down your angry, mean thoughts and feelings (we all have them) in a private journal—but only if you promise to keep it private. Don't be afraid if you find yourself feeling and thinking terrible thoughts—thoughts you never thought you'd have. Because that's all they are: thoughts. You aren't doing or saying anything or hurting anyone. You are simply venting—getting those thoughts out of your head and onto a piece of paper. No accidentally placing it where your husband will see it, though. No writing it on the computer and accidentally leaving the document open. Vent your angers and hurts in a letter addressed to him, reread the letter, feel the release of getting everything out of your system. Then run the letter through a shredder. You will feel much calmer and lighter after you do.

2. Evaluate his exterior. First impressions have an impact when it comes to deciding whether a house or a partner might be purchase or marriage material. Appearances count. But study after study confirms that in human relationships, what women and men find attractive involves more than mere surface physical appearance. (Yes, it's true for men, too.) A woman may notice a man's blue eyes and the cute gap between his teeth, but it's the sparkle and intelligence she sees in those eyes and the way she sees those teeth flash in that darling, goofy grin that probably really attracted her. She may like a man's height or build or strong hands, but it's the way he uses those hands to lift her face toward his and the way he draws her close to his chest when he kisses her that make her fall in love. Think back to when you fell in love with your husband. Ask yourself what it was about his exterior and the qualities and spirit animating him that made you decide he's "the one."

Try this: The next time you're at a party or family gathering, move away from your husband and observe him from a distance when he doesn't know you're watching and is just being his natural self. What do you see? His physique may not be as trim as when you first met and his hair may be thinner, but otherwise? He's the same man you fell in love with. Imagine you weren't married to him and didn't know everything you do know about what living with him is like. Would you be attracted? When my clients do this exercise, their answer is usually yes. The old spark sparkles still.

3. Tour the interior. Outside appearances matter, but nobody buys a house after looking at it from only the outside. A house can look well maintained on the outside and be a snake pit within, or it can look a lot smaller or roomier, darker or cheerier on the outside than it actually is. The same is true of people. Many men and women have had the experience of thinking someone was attractive until they got to know the person better and discovered how selfish or angry or untrustworthy or egotistical the person was. By the same token, many women have told me that when they first met their husband they thought he was pleasant-looking, sure, but not especially attractive until they got to know him—what he cared about, what he believed in, how he treated people and lived his life. The more they got to know him, the more attractive he became, until, by the time of the wedding, in their eyes he was the handsomest man in the world.

How attractive is your husband's interior? Is there a huge heart snuggled inside that barrel chest? Does he do your widowed mother's taxes without being asked *and* let her come on vacation with you to Italy? Is he sometimes gruff and grumpy on the outside, but you know there's nothing he wouldn't do for you or the kids? Does he insist you go back to school even if it means reducing the household income, because he knows that's what you long to do? Does he give you room to walk around in the relationship, be yourself, have your moods and opinions, pursue your interests, choose your friends?

Try this: Carry a notebook and pen in your purse, and every time your husband says or does even the smallest thing that makes you like or admire him, make a mental note of it, then write it down when he's not around. Every time you remember something generous or thoughtful he did for you or anyone else in the past, write that down, too. No negatives. Just positives. Keep it up for a week. Although it may seem silly at first, see if you don't feel more appreciative of him when the week is through.

4. Check the construction. A house can look good outside and in, but if it's made of cheap material and was thrown up in a hurry, it's unlikely to look good for long. The normal wear and tear that a better-constructed house easily withstands can leave a more cheaply constructed house looking shabby. Shoddy construction and materials can also translate into greater structural damage when heavy rains or high winds strike. A sturdy house is reliable. It resists the elements. It withstands the test of time. Similarly, human beings differ in the quality of their moral construction and ethical fiber. What have years of living with your husband revealed about his?

Try this: Ask yourself: Is your husband a liar? Is he a gambler? Does he have a problem with substance abuse? Has he ever been unfaithful? Has he ever abandoned you or the kids? Does he cheat or steal? Has he ever been abusive? If the answer to these questions is no, consider yourself fortunate—and think about how the problems you're having stack up against problems such as these. If the answer is yes, there is still help for you. But not in this chapter. Turn immediately to the Appendix: FEMA for Relationships, at the back of the book, and read it carefully. Later, there will be time to return here, but first things first.

Now ask yourself another series of questions: Is your husband reliable and trustworthy? Is he a good father? Does he contribute to the household income? Is he honest enough and ethical enough, generous and kind enough, most of the time? Does he respect you, recognizing your contributions to the family? Is he there for you when you really need him, and do you know in your heart that as long as he lives and breathes, he always will be (except during playoffs)? Do you know he really loves you and really tries to make you happy—even though his underwear lands on the floor every day? If your answers to these questions are a lot more yeses than nos, ask yourself one more question: Are you sure your relationship is as bad as you sometimes think it is?

On the other hand, you may have picked up this book because you can't feel these positive emotions coming from him anymore. You're too angry. He's too angry. You are sure the love has died. You are sure your husband does not respect you, perhaps does not even acknowledge you appropriately. This, of course, is why we call it the devaluation stage—because feelings and behaviors shift to a place of thinking your partner isn't worth the trouble. Many couples enter my office feeling exactly this way! As scary as it may be, I urge you to slow down and keep reading. Because sometimes we can feel what we are sure is actual hatred for a partner, and in that moment we can be certain that things will never change. However, almost always they do. The Appendix will offer you reassurance that if you don't feel better and calmer and more positive after you read this book, there are still steps you can take to save your marriage. In my office, couples who feel this way frequently just need to talk, vent, and develop better tools for marriage. They need to repair or reconstruct the dynamic between them. These couples, when they start to feel better with and about each other, are often shocked at how low their feelings can swing, how sure they can feel that relief will never arrive—and then it does.

5. Comparison-shop. In the world of home buying and selling, protocol recommends researching the market—discovering what is out there that meets a buyer's minimum requirements and is also within her price range, as well as checking to see how the price that sellers hope to get compares to those of comparable houses. The bottom line: Buyers often find that they wanted champagne housing but have a beer budget, and sellers learn that they don't live in a palatial Trump building after all, and they'll need to accept a lower bid.

Financial advisors often wisely recommend, in fact, that people looking to sell and then buy ask themselves a key question when looking at homes that have sold for roughly the price they're hoping to get for theirs: If they had to choose between the home they own and the one they're looking at, which would they select? I encourage couples who are considering ending their marriage to do a similar kind of market research—not by going out and shopping for a potential new spouse (though they may hope that's what I mean), but by comparing what they know about the pluses and minuses, and strengths and weaknesses of their spouse and marriage to what they know about the problems that their female friends, siblings, and other relatives are dealing with in their marriages.

Many years ago, I used to get together regularly with my three close girlfriends, Denise, Mia, and Faith, to talk and let our hair down as close women friends do. During one of these gatherings it happened that we were all fed up with our husbands at the same time. When one of us started to vent, it was like a dam breaking. Swearing to keep one another's confidences, we all spilled our guts and revealed things we'd never told anyone before. I was shocked by some of the things my friends revealed about their relationships, as I'm sure they were about some of the things I revealed about mine.

We had never complained so much, laughed so hard, or gone home feeling more grateful that we were returning to our own husbands and marital problems instead of one another's.

Try this: Consider your women friends' marital problems. Think about the bad blind date stories your unmarried friends have told you over the years. Think seriously about what they have had to deal with and what you are facing—and then ask yourself this set of questions:

- "Do I really want to trade my problems for theirs, or is that just what I'm thinking now?"
- "Is the grass really greener over there?"
- "Could it be that *all* of us have to go through this, and I was wrong to think it was just my husband and me?"
- "Is it possible that every marriage poses challenges, and I've been so caught up in mine that I didn't realize it?"
- "Was I really happier ten years ago, or does it only seem that way now?"

6. Get a fresh perspective. Often after homeowners have been living in a house for a certain number of years, they can get so used to everything about it that they don't really notice or appreciate what they have anymore. Instead of seeing a wonderful wood-burning fireplace in the living room, they see the ashes in the grate—until a visitor comments on how lucky they are to have that fireplace. Instead of admiring the beautiful claw-foot tub in the master bath, they see the unsightly chips in the enamel—until a girlfriend exclaims over what a beautiful antique tub it is.

The same can be true in marriage. A woman's appreciation for what she has with her husband can be dulled by familiarity and clouded by frustration over his flaws. What you call your husband's "lazy ass," another woman who sees him through a less tarnished lens might call his "cute butt" or "laid-back charm." If that's what you used to call it, too, but haven't for a long while, it may be time to step back and try to see him again the way other people do.

Parties can be good places to do this kind of observing, as one couple I was counseling discovered when they attended the husband's office Christmas party. Frank was a civil engineer, a field that his wife, Laura, knew little and, to be honest, cared less about. In one session she had cracked, nastily, that if she were told she had only a week to live, she'd want to spend it all with Frank because he'd make it seem like five years—he was *that* boring. At the party, though, watching him surrounded by colleagues and staff who shared his passion and respected his expertise, Laura saw a whole different side of her husband. Standing in a group with all eyes and attention focused on him, he was engaged, alive, animated, at ease, funny, witty, well-spoken. Laura couldn't believe it was the same man. Later, in the ladies' room, a young female engineer came up to her and gushed, "I just have to tell you what an honor it is to work for your husband. He is *so* wonderful." Repeating this story during our session, Laura glanced sideways at Frank when she got to that part of the story. Frank shrugged modestly, but he looked pleased, and there was a sparkle in Laura's eyes that I hadn't seen before. It took a roomful of strangers (cute, young, female strangers, at that) to get Laura to step back and see Frank in a different light. She became aware that she was clinging to her disappointments of the past because she was afraid to let go of them and see Frank more positively—because she was afraid of being hurt again. When she was able to perceive that fear and articulate it in my office, she also was able to begin letting go of her anger and start taking a fresh look at the guy sitting next to her. Sure, there was work to do, but she began the process of freeing herself to do it.

Try this: In the same notebook you're carrying around to jot down things your husband says or does that make you like him, earmark another section for jotting down every nice thing you hear anyone say *about* him—to him, to you, or to some other third party. Whenever you recall a compliment someone paid him in the past, write that down, too. Call or have coffee with someone you trust who knows and loves you and your husband and wants your marriage to be happy. Ask her: "Susie, remind me why I married Al again, will you? I mean it. I need a refresher course. Tell me everything you can think of that makes him special." Make clear that you're not looking for a phony pep talk; you're asking her to help you get a fresh perspective on your husband's genuine good qualities and strengths. Pluses only. No minuses. The minuses you can come up with yourself.

7. Weigh the contingencies. Sometimes homeowners who've been thinking of selling will get caught up in the frenzy of a hot housing market and decide they have to sell now, immediately, to get top dollar for their house. Some get so bent on cashing in quickly that they sell without having another home to move into. Instead they may move into a rental home that they don't really like and costs more than they wanted to pay, but they take it anyway because they need a place in a hurry. It's only temporary, they tell themselves. Often, though, they end up living in this limbo state for much longer than planned as their cash reserves get eaten away by rent, monthly fees on all the furniture they had to put in storage, and a thousand other expenses they didn't anticipate. Some of these impulse sellers may still be glad they sold their house when they did if

children. Kids like routine, familiarity, security. Moving to a new house, neighborhood, and school can be traumatizing. To minimize disruption, parents often postpone selling and relocating until the end of the school year or until the kids start high school or until the kids are in college or off on their own. If your children are young and your marriage, however unsatisfying it may be at the moment, presents no threat to any family member's health and safety, I urge you to think further—for your children's sake, if nothing else. Couples often sit in my office and tell me how unhappy they are and how their kids want them to be happy and how the kids will be happier if their parents are happier, even if that means getting a divorce. The truth is, kids care about their *own* happiness, and, short of an abusive situation, having a mom and dad in the same house is what makes kids feel happy and safe. Children shouldn't be expected to care about the quality of their parents' conversations or if they have a good sex life. In fact, once kids are old enough to know what sex is, they prefer to think their parents have *no* sex life! Kids don't want anything to change in a reasonably calm and stable home, unless it changes for the better for *them*. That's normal childhood development, and it's how you want your kids to feel. In fact, if your kids are absorbed with your problems instead of theirs, it's not a good sign, because the best-case scenario is that a kid shouldn't have to deal with such difficult adult issues until she herself is an adult.

That said, children don't want to see their parents fight, either. They want their parents to act like adults and work out their stuff so the kids can relax and actually get to experience and enjoy that one short, carefree time most human beings ever get in life: childhood.

Try this: 1.) Watch your children. They should be wrapped up in their own lives, not yours. 2.) Consider how you and your husband would handle shared custody of the children and what that would demand of them: being shuttled back and forth between homes; never knowing where their stuff is and realizing too late that they left something they need the next day, like their homework, at the other house. The stress children experience going back and forth between two households is enormous. 3.) Keep in mind that when parents divorce, eventually (not immediately but eventually) the children often have a better and stronger relationship with one parent, and they pull away (or are moved away) from the other parent—usually their father. Several studies confirm this sad truth. Do you really think that your kids will think they are better off without their dad? Even if you do think so now, later in their lives, this will be a hole in the fabric of their childhood and development that is hard to fill. As novelist Peter de Vries once said, "The bonds of matrimony are like any other bonds. They mature slowly."

9. Remember the rules of investing. In real estate, as in most other investments, the general rule is that although cash values may rise and fall over the short term, over the long term, barring some cataclysmic event, values are pretty much guaranteed to rise. Marriage works the same way. Over the short term, there will be ups and downs, peaks and valleys, periods of volatility and long lulls. But in the long term, the investment in marriage almost always pays off. In fact, it's probably one of the most secure long-term investments two people can make.

If you are in a lull or valley in the book value of your marriage right now, think ahead. Over the course of a long-term relationship, partners will naturally move apart and come back together, move apart and come back together. What can look like a crisis in the short term often reveals itself over the long term to be what it really is: nothing more than a part of the natural ebb and flow, highs and lows of married life.

Try this: Think back to when you were a kid and had a really bad fight with a parent or sibling and swore to yourself, absolutely meaning it, that you were never, ever, ever going to speak to that parent or sibling again. Ever. Recall how many times you felt that way intensely and how many times that feeling inevitably passed. Whatever you are experiencing in your marriage at the moment, trust me, if you hang in there and do the work necessary for improvement—or, for more trivial problems, allow time to take its course—things *will* improve.

10. Don't underestimate sentimental value. When homeowners sell and leave a house, they leave behind more than the physical structure: walls, floors, windows, rooms. They also leave a part of their family history and the memories of the family occasions and life events that took place in that house: the pencil marks on the kitchen doorframe that charted the children's growth; the laughably ugly chandelier in the dining room that was a couple's first home improvement purchase—and how sophisticated they thought it was then; the rose bushes they planted and tended so carefully that now bloom in full glory every June. When husbands or wives abandon a marriage, they leave big parts of their history behind, too. And once it's gone, it's gone. And the deep ache comes later—when the anger wears off, the pain sets in.

Try this: Walk through your home, room by room, recalling precious family moments that occurred in each one. Remember that only last week your husband spent hours sitting at the kitchen table with your daughter, helping her with her math homework with a tenderness that was palpable. Remember one Saturday a few months ago, when he walked into the kitchen very upset that the barber had cut his hair too short, and it took fifteen minutes to convince him to go grocery shopping with you without a hat. Remember when he sat on the edge of the tub in the master bathroom while you knelt on the floor with your head over the toilet bowl, because you were so nauseous from morning sickness during your first pregnancy and he didn't want to leave you alone. Remember how, one night last month, he reached out for you in bed and grabbed you and hugged you for dear life while he was sound asleep and having a bad dream. Remember the next morning, when he got down on his hands and knees, completely naked, to look under the bed for a shoe, and you saw his ominously large and terribly pale butt swaying from side to side in the air and couldn't stop laughing. Be very sure you understand this: If you leave the marriage, you walk away from all that history, all those years of loving, all those years of rooting for each other. No matter what kinds of bad memories you have now, the good ones will surface, and don't you want to be with him when they do?

11. Know your real needs. Some homeowners love visiting show homes and going on house tours to get a glimpse of how other people live and to fantasize about what it would be like to live the way they do, in such modern, spacious, expensive, luxurious, exquisitely decorated homes. Sometimes homeowners will come back with ideas for spiffing up their own home: "If we extended the porch and put a pond in over there . . ." Other times, though, if they're feeling fed up with all the problems and flaws in their house, they may come back from these tours even more convinced that their own house is a dump. In this state of heightened emotion, they often overlook the fact that the fancy home they just visited doesn't really suit their tastes or lifestyle at all. Oh sure, all that white carpeting makes a big impression, but they wouldn't want to live in a house where they'd have to make visitors take off their shoes before entering and where the children, let alone the dog, could never be allowed in the living room, much less on the couch. Yes, those glass walls let in a lot of light, but the heating bills would be enormous.

Sometimes, when spouses are going through a rough time together, they start thinking that maybe they would be happier in a different kind of marriage that, in reality, wouldn't suit them at all. A husband might start thinking he'd like his wife to quit her job and stay home and cook for him every day, but he's forgetting that his wife loves her job and staying home would make her miserable. Moreover, this would make him the family's sole breadwinner, a burden he's more than happy to share. A woman might fantasize about being married to a titan of industry like one of the other school moms is, forgetting that Sunday morning last summer when she had breakfast in a diner with her girlfriends and watched a family of four in the booth across from them. The husband had that perfectly groomed and put-together look of a business big-shot, which he must have been, because as his wife and children ordered and ate their breakfast, he talked business on his cell phone during *the entire meal*. The whole scene made her want to grab that cell phone and throw it out the window. Here's the thing: There's a reason you married the man you did and not some other man, and that reason is that, on some level, it was the right match, the right fit. And underneath all your current dissatisfactions, it likely still is.

Try this: Try to set aside all your complaints and dissatisfactions with your husband for a moment—not forever, for the moment— and try to remember some of the things about this man and this marriage that make them just right for you. One female client of mine couldn't get off the subject of her husband's incompetence at doing laundry (he always ruined something, and she was sure he did it on purpose to get off the hook in the future) until he brought up the long, luxurious foot rubs he gave her while they watched television in the evening. Another wife went on a tear about how tired she was of her husband playing golf every Saturday and leaving her home with the kids, until I gently reminded her of things she had said earlier about what a wonderful stepfather he had been to those children—making happy family occasions, for example, of every birthday their real father missed, which was pretty much all of them. She blushed and admitted, "That's true, I've been forgetting that."

12. Remember what matters most. The three most critical factors in determining the value of real estate are: location, location, location. The same is true in marriage. If your husband's head is on the pillow next to yours every night, your marriage, right there, is worth a lot.

Here's the bottom line, which can never be repeated too often: After the honeymoon ends, all homes and all marriages need work. The purpose of conducting this appraisal is to inspire and motivate you to want to do that work by helping you to have a better sense of how valuable your marriage really is. The point is to get you to step back from any pain, hurt, or anger you may be feeling and recognize, again, that you are married to a good person with whom you could build a better relationship. Even if he looks like Cyrano de Bergerac, he's *your* Cyrano. There was a time when you loved him more than anything. *That guy you fell in love with is still there. And those feelings are still there.* They can be reignited if you're willing to try.

You don't have to feel all warm and fuzzy about your husband right now. You simply have to hold on to the awareness that he's a decent human being and that there's more good, worth, and potential in your marriage than you were perhaps giving him or yourself credit for.

In truth, that's enough reason to try to repair and revitalize your marriage. Even if you don't have children, before you give up on your marriage you should feel that you have done everything you could to try to improve it—if for no other reason than to make sure that if you do eventually decide to end it, you won't regret later that you didn't try harder to save it. The reality is that marriage is not for the faint of heart. It's work, and, in my opinion, until you've tried everything, it's too soon to bail out.

Once you complete this appraisal of your marriage and have a better sense of how valuable it is to you, the next step is to do an inspection of its foundation, checking for any deterioration or damage that may not be visible on the surface, and that may need attention before moving on to other renovations and repairs. Chapter 3 will guide you through this inspection, and help you reverse any damage that may have been done over the years.

Grab the Flashlight—You Have a Quick Inspection to Make

Checking for Deterioration or Damage to Your Relationship's Foundation

In the preceding chapter, I walked you through a twelve-step exercise for reappraising your marriage the way a homeowner might reappraise a house. The purpose was to begin to clear away the accumulation of negative debris that clouds your perceptions of your spouse. When things start falling apart in your marriage, it can be hard to remember the strengths and positive attributes of your relationship *and* your partner that exist under that debris, whether you see them, feel them, or believe in them or not. Like reaching for the prize in the Cracker Jack box, we sometimes have to dig deeper than we thought to find these treasures—and get a little messy, too. However, the willingness to do so has its rewards. In my practice, couples are occasionally amazed that they can be so furious or hurtful toward each other, so far from loving each other when they first enter counseling, only to discover later that their anger was the behavior that masked deeper hurts, their deeper fear that if and when they cleared away the debris, they'd find nothing positive. When, instead, they find each other, they can be amazed at how the anger dissolves.

That's why the formal reappraisal of a house or marriage can be the only antidote to the "devaluation" stage, the only accurate measure that reassures a couple as to why they bought or married in the first place. With any luck, the appraisal you did in the last chapter will motivate you to move forward with the work you need to do on your marriage to reach the point where you can take pride in it and appreciate it again.

I'll help you draw up a marriage plan, or "blueprint," for doing that work in Chapter 4. First, though, given how long couples tend to put off dealing with the messes they know about, much less go poking around for other messes they suspect are there but hope to avoid having to address, you need to grab a flashlight now and conduct a quick inspection of the basic underpinnings of your marriage. You can't repair anything without checking for signs of deterioration or damage at the source.

Marriages and Houses Are Both Built on Foundations

Breaking ground is the first step in both home building and relationship building. Both are celebrated occasions, but in a relationship, breaking ground runs deeper than just falling in love. It's when she doesn't flinch upon discovering that he still sleeps with a teddy bear. It's when he tells her they'll figure it out when she lets him know she's terrified to fly. Breaking ground is when two people allow themselves to be deeply vulnerable with each other because they feel they are safe and they are loved—warts and all.

At this point, with a solid piece of land or a solid lover, there is the accelerated desire to build. Yet, to build up, you must first dig down and then pour the foundation. This crucial stage in the construction process has to be done right, because everything, and I do mean everything, is built on top of that. When the foundation is deep, strong, and solid, the house or relationship that rises upon it stands strong in all kinds of weather. A strong foundation in a relationship is what enables it to survive the sorrows, losses, tragedies, and reversals of fortune that are an unavoidable part of life. How good it is to know that the two of you will always stand together as a team, clear in the knowledge that you've built a foundation that remains unshakable.

In home building, that kind of foundation requires some combination of concrete and steel. In marriages, that kind of foundation is built on trust: when she doesn't throw the teddy bear back at him in anger, when he doesn't humiliate her about her fear of flying, when you feel the most vulnerable parts of you are safe in your partner's hands and you know your partner is rooting for you, rooting for the marriage. This is what we're going to examine in this chapter: the trust you and your husband have in your marriage and each other. In a world full of surprises that can range from tornados to your sister-in-law throwing her husband out and sending him to live with you, couples need to do all they can to make sure the foundation of trust in their marriage remains stronger than the stressors that are likely to test it. Because it *will* get tested. All marriages do.

Four Signs That Something's Starting to Give

As long as the house remains standing, most homeowners don't spend much time thinking about the foundation. They just kind of assume it will do its job—until it doesn't. Somehow, they don't think to check for deterioration or damage until a wide crack appears in a ceiling beam, or the dog drops her ball on the kitchen floor and it rolls into a corner and the homeowners realize that the floor, once level, no longer is.

Like houses, relationships start to shift and crack if we don't pay attention. However, if we do pay attention, signs of this kind of trouble are everywhere and generally take the form of reduced connectedness. Trust and good connection are qualities that can't be separated. Spouses who trust each other show their connectedness on a daily basis. It's found in the warmth of their conversations, that simple touch on her shoulder when he passes by. When trust diminishes, a husband and wife may stop paying attention to each other and start withholding intimacy and affection, passively or actively withdrawing from a partner or pushing a spouse away. Some of the ways this kind of damage often manifests itself are:

Letting appearances go. When trust begins to erode, spouses will sometimes relax or abandon their former standards of grooming, hygiene, and dress, making themselves less attractive, consciously or unconsciously keeping each other at a distance. One former female client of mine with a high-level job in the cosmetics industry never walked out her front door looking anything less than perfectly groomed and sharply dressed. On weekends, though, the time she and her husband would spend quietly and, in the past, romantically together, she'd stop showering and brushing her teeth. She would put on her sweatpants on Friday night and leave them on until Monday morning. She came to see me not because of this, but because she felt depressed. Eventually what she figured out was that she was angry at her husband for all kinds of slights that had been building up for a very long time. But instead of talking with him, she'd been second-guessing herself, thinking, "I'm too hard on him" or "He just had a bad day" or "Why am I always dissatisfied?" or "All I need is a good night's sleep." Turning her anger inward instead of putting her anger into words, she acted it out, keeping him as far away from her as possible. When she found the language to tell him the ways he was hurting her, she was also able to tell him that her weekend behavior had been her effort to communicate that message. While her husband wasn't thrilled to hear this, he was relieved to gain some understanding of her shift in behavior. He wanted his wife back, after all, and this conversation represented the first step in helping them figure out how to reconnect.

Altering bedtime rituals. When spouses go from sliding into bed together each night to one of them always staying up late or going to bed early, that's not a good sign. When they switch from always climbing in bed naked or minimally clad to enjoy the touch of each other's skin to one or both coming to bed wrapped in flannel—that's also a pretty clear signal that something's wrong. It would probably be a good idea for the spouse who feels shut out (because that spouse *is* being shut out) to gently and calmly try to find out what's going on. Yet you'd be surprised how long two people can go before one of them says something about it.

Nota bene: Conflicting job schedules sometimes make crawling into bed together impossible. But when they do, couples with strong foundation-maintenance skills will often find an extra moment to hug, to linger, to awaken their partner to kiss good-bye.

Avoiding and evading. In some cases husbands and wives will disregard established mealtime rituals and start eating dinner before their partner comes home, or away from the table when both partners are home, sometimes even preferring to eat standing in the kitchen rather than sitting with their spouse. Or they call at the last minute to say they're having dinner with a friend.

Other husbands and wives simply stop interacting with their partner on anything more than a perfunctory level. They say things like "Did you take out the garbage?" or "Did my mother call?" in a voice that sounds more like "screw you" than anything else. They may isolate themselves from their mate by reading, watching television, being busy with the kids, or talking on the phone—saving all the best parts of themselves and sharing them with everyone but their spouse.

Exaggerated anger. When trust is damaged, spouses erupt over minor slights and offenses. Any reason or no reason will do. Say that a couple is dressing for a dinner party. The wife steps back from the bathroom mirror in her stocking feet to check her makeup, lands right on a wet towel her husband left on the bathroom floor, and flips out because now her foot is wet. Or say her husband finally learned not to leave wet towels on the floor. Instead, he left this one on the toilet seat. Say the wife sees it there and erupts because, damn, is it really so hard after six years in the house to locate the hamper? Clearly, something more serious than wet towels is fueling her rage.

In my practice, I see this kind of out-of-proportion anger between spouses almost every day. During one session, Mariko could not get off the point that whenever she sent her husband, Sammy, grocery shopping with a written list of everything she needed for dinner, he always managed to forget something. Always. With a written list right in his hand! After five years of marriage, she fumed, you'd think he would have learned to go over the list before getting in the checkout line. He *clearly* didn't care about her enough to take the extra thirty seconds to do so. Now, this was the same Sammy who worked his buns off in his first job as a CPA *and* took on a second part-time job to save the money for the down payment on the town house the family was able to buy in Queens. This is the same Sammy who is home by six thirty every evening, and who, when he walks through the door, takes their two toddlers off Mariko's hands. He watches and plays with them while Mariko, a financial analyst temporarily turned stay-at-home mom, makes supper. He bathes them and puts them to bed. He sits with them in the middle of the night when they have tummy aches or nightmares. He not only remembers Mariko's birthday and their anniversary, he remembers the day they met, the night they first said they loved each other, the song they first danced to, and her favorite gemstone, color, and flower. And Mariko is ready to ditch Sammy over a quart of milk, a can of crushed tomatoes, a large jar of mayonnaise, and a box of elbow macaroni.

The groceries aren't the real issue here, of course. They are the escape hatch for Mariko's anger about something else. What? She's not sure yet or isn't ready to say. However, it's clear that something basic, and it's not a food group, is deteriorating. Maybe Mariko doesn't feel respected or heard or recognized or valued in the marriage in some very deep and essential way. Maybe being home with two toddlers all day is too much for her. Maybe she feels that Sammy thinks she's got it easy, doesn't understand what her everyday life is like now. Whatever the truth is, she feels he has broken his connection with her, and thus, broken trust.

The "Same or Separate Rooms" Exercise

Checking for Damage and Distance Couples Can't See

I use a simple exercise in my office to gauge how well the foundation of trust in a couple's marriage is holding up. You can do this exercise yourself to measure the strength of your foundation. All you need is a large piece of plain paper, a pen or pencil, and two coins.

Step 1: Draw a big square on the sheet of paper. The square represents the "house" of your marriage.

Step 2: Place the coins inside the square. They represent you and your husband. Position them to reflect how close you felt to him when you were newlyweds.

Step 3: Reposition the coins to reflect how close you feel now.

This simple exercise usually reveals a painful truth, the truth that has usually prompted one member of a couple to phone me for a first appointment: The distance between them has grown. One man actually tried to place his coin in another zip code (by walking out of my office and into my waiting room with his coin). That is how far apart from his wife he felt. One female client didn't just move the coins far apart. She took a pen and drew a line down the middle of the paper, dividing it in half. As far as she was concerned, there wasn't just more emotional space between her and her husband in the house of their marriage now; they were now living in separate dwellings.

When spouses are not actively engaged in shoring up the foundation of trust between them by talking and listening, airing their dreams and hopes, asking questions, appreciating each other's efforts, exploring their partner's imperfections, trying to find ways to work through differences and honor each other's needs—in other words, actively maintaining their connection—they are heading in the other direction, whether they know it or not. They are actively neglecting and thus eroding their connection. It doesn't matter whether they admit to it or they don't. It doesn't matter whether they have justifiable complaints or they don't. Once they start neglecting their relationship, deterioration sets in rather quickly and they can expect little more than crumble and rot. Whatever they say or don't say, they know it's happening, and like animals sensing an earthquake, they start exhibiting strange behaviors: not brushing their teeth, wearing flannel nightgowns to bed, not getting off the phone when their partner comes home, saying to the children when their partner is in the room, "Tell your father not to forget to close the garage door," not coming home for dinner, retreating to separate rooms in the house of their marriage and closing and sometimes locking the door—because they sense danger. They sense that their marriage is no longer the safe place it once was.

So, if you remember nothing else after reading this chapter, remember this:

People who love each other don't stop talking to each other about things that really matter to them merely because their lives are busy. They stop talking because they feel they can no longer trust their partner to be gentle with and respectful of their truest feelings and dearest dreams.

A client of mine, James, arrived for one session deeply distraught because a friend had invited him to go in on buying and running a small restaurant. A hotel manager and trained chef, James had always dreamed of having his own restaurant. But when he went home giddy with excitement and told his wife about this golden opportunity, she went ballistic: Was he crazy? Quit his job and give up the benefits? Did he have any idea how risky the restaurant business is and how much work it entails? He'd never be home!

The more she ranted, he said, the more the idea of never being home started to appeal to him. But it wasn't her angry initial reaction that upset him so much. He had expected that. He knew how much his job benefits meant to her, especially with their first baby on the way. What hurt him was that after that reaction, she refused to discuss the idea at all. When he brought it up the next day and said, "Look, let's just talk about it, okay?" his wife got up off the couch and left the room. Then she came back and stood in the doorway and said, "That's it, James, I mean it. Not another word. It's insane." That's what really hurt him, he said— that she wouldn't even hear him out. He could accept that she was against it. But it wounded him deeply that she wouldn't even explore the fantasy with him—and that she made him feel foolish for daring to dream. In Chapter 5, I'll review how spouses can avoid trampling on each other's dreams in this unintentionally or intentionally cruel way by conducting what I call an "information-gathering" conversation: learning how to give their partner a chance to talk about dreams and desires, even the ones they may find threatening.

Four Ways to Shore Up a Foundation and Keep It Strong

Inevitably, all spouses step on each other's most tender dreams and feelings in one way or another. It just isn't possible to always be attuned to each other or always to be as sensitive as a situation calls for. Even the most loving, attentive, and well-intentioned spouses are bound to make mistakes—sometimes big ones. There are four rules couples need to follow for dealing with these injuries so that they don't erode the foundation of trust that spouses so depend on from each other:

Rule # 1: When you spot rot in the foundation, you can't keep it to yourself. You have to share.

Many spouses are deeply reluctant to simply talk to each other because they're afraid that if they let themselves feel, much less try to express, how hurt they are, they won't be able to stop once they've started. They'll fall apart or they'll be further rejected. Certainly it is wise to consider such outcomes; they could happen and, perhaps, have happened in the past. In Chapter 6, I'll discuss how it can sometimes be that spouses will start talking, get meaner as they go on, and find themselves unable to stop—so if you or your partner have a mean streak, we'll address that soon. As for the other fears— yes, if you're carrying a lot of pain inside you, you might fall apart, it's true. In fact, you probably will. But falling apart can actually be healthy and beneficial in a couple of ways. The scientific evidence that emotional states can affect physical health is overwhelming. Holding in negative emotions can be detrimental to your health, and letting them out in healthy way, such as by crying, can be beneficial. If you have been stuffing your hurt and sadness so far down inside you that your husband—who, I grant you, may not be paying the closest attention—doesn't know you've been carrying these feelings around, then breaking down lets him know in no uncertain terms how much you've been hurting. And that's good. Because it gives him a chance to react and respond—and however he does, positively or negatively, you've started the work on your marriage. Moreover, if your fear is that you'll be rejected, that your partner won't respond, it's more of a reason, not less of one, to address your hurt. If you don't take care of making your needs known, they never will be, and you're acting as if you're a nobody and your needs don't matter. Thus you are simply rejecting yourself before he has the chance.

Keep in mind: You're not Humpty-Dumpty. You're not going to break into a million pieces and stay broken. Eventually you will calm down and put yourself back together again. And you'll probably feel much lighter because you've just unloaded the heavy weight of words that needed to be said. You may even feel more peaceful and more energetic. It takes a huge amount of energy day after day to fit twenty pounds of anger in a ten-pound bag. (If that's what you've been doing, it's no wonder you've been feeling so tired!) Moreover, try not to rush the "putting yourself back together" process. As I tell my clients, the confusion, pain, and anxiety they experience when they surrender control over these deep hurts aren't pleasant, but they're the necessary precursor to the all-important next stage, which is to begin taking a serious look at what isn't working in their marriage.

Additionally, a number of studies on "resilience"—the trait that enables people and marriages to triumph over setbacks and adversities—have found that people who fall apart when it's appropriate to do so come back stronger and better prepared for future troubles than people who refuse to let themselves fall apart. Refusing to fall apart can be a sign that not only are you not taking your feelings seriously, but that you are unwilling to deal with the way things are. Falling apart puts you in the present and in the middle of the action instead of keeping you stuck in wishing for the past, pretending things are okay, or hoping they will magically repair themselves in the future. Falling apart (as long as you remember to feed the kids) may be the best thing you can do.

Rule # 2: No hanging a painting over a hole in the wall and calling it fixed.

Feeling unsafe with a spouse, the person you rightfully expect to feel most safe with, doesn't happen after a single incident of being slighted, criticized, or even humiliated. It takes more, usually *a lot* more, to reach that danger zone. Therefore, once that feeling and the accompanying anger and vulnerability come, the guilty spouse who did the hurting, however unintentionally, will need to invest time and effort into repairing the damage done. Spouses do this by letting their partners know that, whether they were aware they were causing pain or they weren't, whether they violated the contract of trust by mistake or on purpose, however it happened they take full responsibility for their actions.

If your spouse expresses this kind of pain and anger toward you, don't even think a simple "I'm sorry" or "I didn't do it on purpose" is enough. This is the time for you to say:

This was my fault.

I screwed up.

I make no excuses.

I'm not asking you to forgive me now.

I'm asking you to think about what you need from me to repair the damage I did.

Of course, there is every chance that *you* are the one who is hurting, that *you* want your husband to say these words to *you*. And he should. Yet it's most likely to happen if you set a good, positive model for him by fessing up when you screw up. It won't happen the first or second time, because it will take him a while to notice.

However, if you begin to accept responsibility face-to-face for your own actions, you may find that he is much more able to step up to the plate himself. Be patient. If he's going to learn from example, let it be your good one.

I'll talk more in subsequent chapters about what couples need to do to avoid the kinds of intentional hurts and breakage that can lead to divorce, and how to address them when they happen. For the purposes of this chapter, where we acknowledge that the foundation of trust is cracked, this is the only way to begin to make repairs—no matter what the guilty partner may think.

The Trouble with "I'm Sorry"

I recently saw an ad on the Internet by someone offering to tell people the "one little thing" they needed to do to improve their marriage for only $39.95—guaranteed to work or their money back. Of course, the ad didn't reveal what that "one little thing" was. For all I know, people who bit and paid money got a recipe for "forgiveness cookies"—if they got anything at all. What struck me about the ad, though, was the advertiser's faith, probably well founded, that people would bite: that there are people who believe there is "one little thing" that can work instant improvements on their marriage and *all other marriages*—like some miracle detergent or stain remover. What a lovely fantasy!

And yet, in my experience, people view that other miracle marriage spot-remover—"I'm sorry"—the same way. One quick application and—presto!—hurt feelings disappear. Good as new! But it's never that simple. We're not wash-and-wear people; we're not made out of polyester fabric, so we can just shake off the wrinkles or the hurt. Think of how often your partner has said. "I'm sorry" to you clearly hoping that it would signal the end of the matter, and it didn't. Think of how often *you* have said "I'm sorry" to him after a bad fight and *meant* it, and it still didn't help either of you feel better because the hurts caused by mean words you didn't mean to say, the ones that flew out of your mouth, went too deep to be instantly healed.

On the other hand, it is possible for the smallest of gestures, if they're sincere, quickly applied, and feel like authentic responses and not pat platitudes, to be amazingly effective.

During one session a few years ago, a woman named Anita spoke tearfully about fearing that her husband was only going through the motions of their marriage, and that spending time with her was but one more motion he went through—that he felt nothing for her. There was nothing specific however, that she could pick up on. Even asking for something as simple as sitting together to watch a movie on a Saturday evening, she said, was met with a look of annoyance as Al, her husband, retreated into his office, where he seemed to spend more and more time. "Look, I'm sorry," Al responded, with an edge in his voice, sounding like he'd said the same words a million times before and launching into his "Do you have any idea of what I'm going through" routine.

"Time out," I said, "Can you look at Anita," I asked Al. Anita went to speak, and I raised my hand to my lips, signaling her *not* to talk. After some awkward seconds, Al lifted his face and looked at his wife. " 'I'm sorry' doesn't seem to be working," I said gently. "Can you think of something that might work better?" Anita was weeping. I handed him a box of tissues so that the tissue would come from him and not me. As he went to give her one and she looked at him, he started crying as hard as she was. He said, "I feel like a failure. I'm not getting that promotion. I get too wrapped up in my work and it gets me nowhere." He looked at his wife. "But even when I do, I still love you." And then he squeezed her hand tightly.

I wish I could tell you that it always happens this way, but it doesn't. Some partners, just like some stubborn old beams that have shifted off-center, require more work and more pressure, more pushing, more pain. But whether it's couples or individuals who come into my office, it seems that, whatever they come in for, they all want to feel more loved in a way that feels secure. Being denied this love brings out the worst in all of us.

Rule #3: No making a federal case over every little scratch in the plaster.

All partners and all marriages have their good days and their bad days. On good days, husbands and wives cut each other slack when they feel annoyed, even when the irritant is significant, such as when one partner welshes on his or her share of housework or childcare— something that, on any other average day, would trigger, at the very least, an edgy exchange or two. On a bad day, no irritation or annoyance seems too piddling to argue over and even the most trivial oversight can get magnified into a crisis.

During one session, Carla entered my office venting about Bill's habit of leaving the television in the den on all day on weekends, even when he wasn't in the room. "I swear I'm going to get a hammer and smash the television," she said before going on about it for another fifteen minutes. I thought hers was a pretty extreme reaction to a fairly minor offense, but Bill seemed completely unfazed. He sat back and let her get it out of her system. He knew better than I did that this was a no-fight fight. This was Carla being Carla on a bad day.

Sometimes, one spouse will start venting, and the other is wise enough to remain unruffled, knowing there is no deep or important reason for it. The cranky spouse is just blowing off steam over stuff that has nothing to do with his or her partner or the relationship at all. Sometimes it's because of a headache, or husbands and wives are angry about something else, and because their partner really is the person they feel safest with, they take out their bad mood on their mate. It turned out that this is what Carla was doing when she erupted at Bill, using the TV as an excuse. Eventually, she offered that she'd been feeling tense lately because the advertising firm she worked for—which produced TV commercials, by the way—had just lost its two biggest clients and she was starting to worry about her job. Fortunately, Bill knew what was going on at his wife's office, so he hadn't let her outbursts get to him. "She's just feeling stressed," he said, shrugging. I was glad I didn't jump in, although I think it's a very nice idea if a spouse says "Honey, I need to vent for ten minutes" before she starts screaming.

It's a wise spouse who picks his or her battles and doesn't think every eruption of bad temper has to be analyzed and explored, who can recognize when the better course of action is to duck and let the darts whiz past. From time to time we all need a free pass, and when there is trust, a free pass is easy to give . . . now and then.

Rule # 4: Believe your foundation is built to last!

Flying back to New York City from a speaking engagement in Los Angeles a couple of years ago, I had plenty of time to eavesdrop on a conversation between two well-dressed women seated next to each other across the aisle. Early into the flight they discovered that they were both going to New York on business, had both been married for

about four years, and both had preschool-age children they had been
worried about leaving for a few days. Eventually they began comparing notes on their husbands and their marriages, and I became fasci-
nated by the similarities and differences in what they had to say.

The first woman, let's call her Ann, talked about how obsessed
her husband was with football and how abandoned she felt every
time football season rolled around. She confessed, sadly, that her
husband had told her that much as he loved their sixteen-month-old
daughter, he'd be glad when she got older because she was still too
young to have any real fun with. "Can you believe he said that?"
Ann said to her companion, sounding deeply wounded and resentful. "I was just so shocked. I still haven't really forgiven him."

Woman B, let's call her Betty, laughed and said, "Talk about
abandonment! My husband has gotten on this new 'gym kick,'
where he leaves me sound asleep in bed every morning at six AM to
go pump iron down the street. I've started calling him 'Hulk,' just
to mess with him. And get this. The other day, he told me that he
has decided our daughter, Lisa, has finally reached the 'smart pet
stage' where she can at least do basic tricks—sit up, roll over. That
was progress, he said, but he wanted to know how long it would be
before they could have a conversation." "Smart pet stage," she repeated. "So, I handed him the baby and went upstairs to take a bath.
Ten minutes later he came into the bathroom with Lisa crying in his
arms and said, 'I think she's hungry. What should I give her?' So I
said, 'Open a can of Alpo!' " And then Betty cracked up.

What struck me was that the stories these two women had to tell
were so similar, and yet they told them so differently! It was a clas-
sic example of seeing a glass as half empty or half full—of doubting
that the foundation of trust in a marriage could withstand the test of
time and having every confidence that it would.

Some might argue that if these two women had such different attitudes about their husbands and marriages, it must be because for all the surface similarities, there were other, deeper, and more serious qualitative differences. In other words, the woman who seemed less happy and more doubtful must have good reasons to feel that way and the woman who seemed happier and more confident must have good reasons to feel the way she did, too. This is one possible explanation, for sure. But often it's what it looks like: Expect good things in your marriage and you increase your chances of having them. Expect problems, and you can find those, instead. In fact, a school of therapy called cognitive therapy is built on the basic premise that our thoughts, positive and negative, create our feelings. One of the simplest pieces of advice from this school is to start smiling—smile first and the happier feeling will come. Cognitive therapists can produce an ample number of studies that back this up.

What I'm saying is: If you want to increase the likelihood that the foundation of trust between you and your husband will withstand whatever buffeting the house of your marriage may be subjected to, you can start by believing it *will* withstand these stresses and by searching for and focusing on every small shred of evidence to bolster that belief. You can do a lot to shore up the foundation of trust in your marriage by shifting your focus—not all of it, but most of it—away from what is wrong with your husband and marriage to what is right.

I'm not saying that this is easy to do. It isn't—it's one of the first places where those husbands and wives who *hope* their marriage will be happy part ways with those who are willing to *work* to create a happy marriage. Why? Because changing their focus, especially once partners reach the third "devaluation" stage of marriage, is hard work. But what could be more worth working on than a loving and trusting lifelong relationship with a spouse?

PART 2

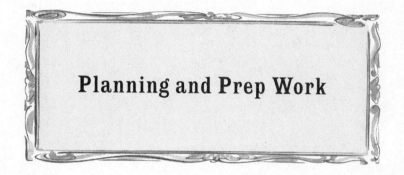

Planning and Prep Work

CHAPTER 4

Think Like an Architect

Create a Blueprint for Your Marriage

In Part 1, we discussed the benefits of learning to view your relationship with new eyes. Before that, you may have felt overwhelmed by the big picture just as a homeowner is when she realizes that she has let a bunch of small repairs go unattended (the leaky faucet that is now a rivulet, the ant or two that is now a platoon, a loose wire that's beginning to hiss), and now she has a much bigger job on her hands. It's not that the problems in your marriage are unmanageable; it's just that they feel unmanageable because you haven't actually done anything except survey them. This chapter begins with the step you take after your assessment, which is to come up with a good, workable plan for how you will tackle making improvements in your marriage, in the same way an architect draws up a plan for building or making improvements to a house.

Before an architect can even begin creating a blueprint, he must first interview the future homeowners about what kind of a house they want—how big, how many rooms, what style and materials, what kind of budget—in order to anticipate and avoid problems before they arise: If the bedroom faces that way, it will miss the morning light; and the deck needs to be bigger if it's going to hold a hot tub and a putting zone.

All these specifications need to be worked out ahead of time, and on paper. After all, future homeowners can't just bring a builder out to a building site, hold up their hands, and say, "The master bedroom should go over there, and I'd like it to be about *yea* big." The blueprint defines the size, shape, width, and depth of a house in detail.

Of course, an architect can execute a perfect blueprint and the project can still hit snags: The homeowners decide they want to add another bedroom, or, upon seeing the way the house comes together on paper, they decide they want the kitchen to face north instead of south. Architects know to expect these kinds of changes, and they keep the early plan somewhat flexible so they can make needed revisions. Eventually, though, everyone agrees, *yes, this is the plan*, and the final blueprint becomes the master document that guides the entire operation. When any member of the construction team has a question or needs clarification, the contractor consults the blueprint. The last thing anyone wants when a house is going up is for the occupants, architect, and builders to be working with different plans!

Like every home construction project, every marriage needs a master plan, too. Not multiple plans: what he wants, what she wants, what his parents want, what her mother wants. Not even two plans: his and hers. Every marriage must have *one joint blueprint* that brings shape to the kind of marriage the partners want now and in the future and the style with which they will discuss concerns. After all, if your husband plans to retire to Florida and you get heat rash, or if you donate 10 percent of your income to charity every year and he thinks that money should go into the kids' college fund, the two of you have some blueprinting to work out.

The best blueprints sketch out all the most important elements of a relationship, such as when spouses will start their family, what their professional goals and ambitions are and how they will try to fulfill them, what their sex lives will be like, how housework will be divvied up, where they will live after they're married, and what kind of lifestyle they dream of for themselves in their futures. Plans can always be changed or modified (and some just fall into place on their own), but partners can't even begin to work toward a shared vision of the future without some preliminary plan to guide them. Spouses who do take time to discuss what kind of marriage they want to create develop a way to talk about values, lifestyles, and dreams in a cooperative fashion. Comparing and combining their individual plans into one shared plan teaches them how to make necessary compromises and stay flexible if future developments require them to change their plan again.

Every Marriage Needs a Plan

Surprisingly, very few couples actually directly discuss an overarching plan before marrying. They'll often float a desire or dream or two: "I want a big family" or "I want to retire to southern California." But they seldom sit down like two architects with a commission and finalize a blueprint. And there's a reason they don't: they're too in love! Who wants to replace a romantic high with rulers and #2 pencils when you can have rose-colored glasses? It's appropriate at this stage, the idealization stage—which some psychotherapists actually call a mini psychosis—to feel that differences, in everything from religion to sleep patterns to beliefs about money, don't matter. If spouses-to-be *didn't* feel that way, if they knew the work ahead, there'd be a lot more test tube babies and a lot fewer ugly bridesmaids' gowns.

Yes, during the idealization phase of love, couples would rather *hope* their plans are compatible than risk discovering that they're not. They'd rather believe that love conquers all—that questions about finances, sex, how many kids they'll have, and whose parents they'll visit for Christmas will just work themselves out.

And, for a while, they do. For months, even years, spouses may not realize that their long-term plans are different. Life is good. Love is strong. Both partners want the same things: lots of time together, lots of sex. For a while, nothing seems worth getting upset about. Because women value harmony so highly, the wife lets annoyances (like a husband deciding he must have the most cutting-edge electronic equipment at all times, even if that means spending a third of his yearly income on gadgets) slide. Because men hate dealing with women's anger, the husband gives in (about spending Thanksgiving at her mother's house, for example, even though he and his mother complain to each other later that his mom hardly ever sees them anymore) and lets his wife have her way to keep the peace. But no two people can keep that up forever. Eventually, both spouses angle to get their own needs met—and here it gets tricky because it can happen at their partner's expense. Both start pushing their separate agendas, or blueprints, not realizing that their blueprints conflict, because they've never compared them. This head-butting leaves them disillusioned and confused. Why is their partner suddenly being so obstinate, so contrary, so dead set on doing or saying or just *assuming* things that are absolutely *not* what the marriage is supposed to be about? Unless one spouse completely steamrolls the other, when couples reach this stage, their marriage-building construction machinery usually gets stuck in the mud because, as my friend Sallie's grandmother once said about marriage, "You can't go north and south at the same time."

Two Plans Equal Trouble

Many of the couples I counsel are caught in exactly this bind. Over the years, I've found that when couples start arguing about sex, time, and money—even though these issues may be quite legitimate—it often boils down to a simple power struggle, born out of a lack of a shared blueprint. Each is trying to have his or her blueprint dominate—each trying to get his or her plan to prevail.

A woman named Samantha, for example, had always planned on quitting her job in human resources to become a stay-at-home mom when she and her husband, Saul, a software designer, started their family. She floated this past Saul when they got married, but having kids seemed so far down the road to him then that he couldn't really focus on it, so he said, sure, that sounded great. Four years later, when Samantha got pregnant, she assumed they both knew she'd quit her job. In the meantime, though, the couple had consciously settled into a comfortable lifestyle that they couldn't possibly sustain on one income, even without a child. Saul figured Samantha knew she'd have to return to work after her maternity leave. Samantha, meanwhile, was thinking about how to reduce expenses so the family could get by on Saul's income. "I think we should sell the boat," she told Saul one day. "I've been looking into what we could get for it." Completely blindsided by this suggestion, Saul flipped out. His blueprint for a happy marriage and family life had always included a boat. That boat was more than a boat to him.

It was the manifestation of his ability to achieve his dreams and deeply connected to his self-esteem. It was like asking him to sell off a part of himself. That's when they came to see me. Saul felt bamboozled and Samantha felt like she was married to a child. They were beginning to realize that they had two different blueprints and it seemed inconceivable to them at that moment that they could figure out how to go forward in a way that would satisfy them both. Their fights were getting out of hand. They hoped, but weren't at all sure, that I could help them figure this out in order to live together happily again.

Many couples reach this kind of impasse in one way or another when they move from the idealization phase of love to the disappointment phase. As you recall, the disappointment phase is when people still think they can change each other, as Samantha believed she could change Saul. "If Saul could only hear what I'm saying about that damn boat," she thought, "he'd understand that selling it is the right thing to do." Somehow, it hadn't occurred to Samantha that Saul could feel just as strongly about a plan for their future that bore no resemblance to hers—except that it also dated back to the idealization phase when, like Samantha, he was sure that all their differences could be easily worked out.

These couples thought so, too:

• Rita sat back in shock during a session in my office when her husband, Uri, mentioned that he'd be inheriting his parents' house in North Carolina when his widowed mother died, and that he wanted the family to move there when he did inherit it. "North Carolina!" Rita said, but when she said it, it sounded more like "Death row! When were you planning on discussing this with me?"

• Theresa, who had always wanted to have three children, was stunned when her husband, Zack, announced shortly after the birth of their second child that he had made an appointment for a vasectomy, because he didn't think they could afford another child and didn't want to take a chance on having one by accident.

• Harry and Donna butted heads over their son's dream of becoming a concert pianist. Harry, who had once studied opera and knew how few people succeed at musical careers, was against it. Donna, who had a beautiful voice and had always wanted to study music but never did, encouraged their son daily.

When partners reach this stage, the ideal scenario would be for them to sit down together in a spirit of trust and goodwill, explore the differences in their marital blueprints, and discuss how to resolve them (or live with them). Perhaps instead of selling the boat, Saul could try to find someone to go in with him as a co-owner. Perhaps Samantha could agree to find work she could do part-time from home after the baby arrives. Perhaps Rita and Uri could agree to start taking family vacations in North Carolina to give Rita and the kids a chance to get to know the area better before making any major decisions about their future. Maybe Theresa could agree to let Zack have a vasectomy if he gives her his word that, if their finances look better in a few years, they'll consider adopting. Maybe Harry and Donna could agree to take a mutual hands-off policy toward their son's career ambitions for a year and, if he still seems serious about it, revisit the subject then.

The truth is that many couples ultimately do find ways to blend their plans. But they can't blend them if they aren't aware of what they are or if they refuse to discuss them. That's why making time to discuss what is important to them now and what they dream of in the future matters so much.

As spouses look for ways to merge/expand/revisit/agree to disagree on the marital blueprint, they should also expect their original plans to end up covered with arrows, erasures, and red circles marking subjects to come back to and problems to resolve next. I warn them to expect such talks to be noisy and possibly even a little heated, with a lot of give-and-take and back-and-forth on both sides.

If you suspect it's time for you and your husband to finally reveal your private marriage blueprints to each other, but you don't know how to initiate this kind of conversation, I suggest starting small with something specific and concrete. Don't hit him with something like "You know, it's time we discussed where our marriage is going." How can he respond to that except by wanting to run out the door? Instead, try something like this: "You know, honey, it struck me yesterday that we've never talked about how we'll pay for Sally's college education. Let's set aside a time to do that because it's been on my mind ever since." Or say, "I know it still seems like a long way off, but I've been thinking lately about what I'd like our retirement to be like. Maybe it's time we started talking and planning." Take it one small, specific step at a time—a point I'll return to later.

If you're nervous about initiating this kind of conversation because you're afraid your blueprint and your husband's will turn out to be so different that you won't be able to find a way to live peacefully after you've come clean, have no fear: The rest of this chapter is dedicated to guiding you through this process, to make it as painless and as productive for the two of you as possible.

Ten Guiding Principles for Sharing and Discussing Your Marital Blueprints

1. Decide what's more important: having a "showcase marriage" or a happy marriage. Couples can't control what fortunes or misfortunes befall them or what areas of agreement or disagreement will arise between them, but they *can* choose to believe in their ability to handle problems and disagreements. They can decide that they *will* find a way to resolve differences about owning a boat or living in North Carolina, even if as yet they have no earthly clue how they're going to do it. This is the difference between romantic love and realistic cooperation, in which spouses make a conscious choice to love, protect, and nurture their life together, even if that means having to wrestle with problems and differences they wish they didn't have to wrestle with, and make compromises and concessions they wish they didn't have to make. Mature love doesn't just involve keeping flexible blueprints; it can mean being ready to throw out those blueprints and start all over if that is what it takes. It means understanding that they may both have to accept and live with things they would prefer not to have to tolerate if the choice were theirs alone, but that they needn't let unhappiness over those specific imperfections in their marriage spoil their happiness with so much else about it that's right and good. Spouses who are able to make this conscious decision to be happy have an easier time accepting other difficult but essential truths about marriage as well. They understand that differences cannot always be reconciled and problems cannot always be resolved—sometimes at all, much less to both partners' satisfaction. They are able to accept that both may have to learn to live together without coming to agreement on an important issue, without getting their way about something that is very important to them. They won't like it when these things happen any more than another couple does; the difference is that they decide they won't let these inevitable times of personal dissatisfaction ruin their marriage or their life.

Partners who are just leaving the idealization stage of marriage, who have yet to actually confront and work through a serious area of disagreement, often confuse this process of negotiation and compromise with "settling" or "lowering their standards and expectations." What I'm talking about here, however, is cooperation—the mature, enlightened behaviors that produce less self-absorption, more closeness, and a deeper love as part of a solid, working, adult relationship. Spouses who insist on sticking with their individual, original blueprints may build a lifestyle that suits them exactly, but it's not a marriage—it's a lifestyle for one. Spouses who are veterans of this process, on the other hand, know that sometimes they have to be prepared to adjust to concessions they don't want to accept, and not just easy ones. Uri has to accept that his wife and children might hate North Carolina. Theresa has to accept that she may never have a third child.

Perhaps you can't imagine making concessions as large as these. Your wish may be to meld your plan and your husband's plan in ways that don't require such significant sacrifices on either side. All couples wish for that, but few marriages are so blessed. In reality, marriage requires making difficult compromises and concessions over and over again.

2. Toss the plans for the prefab. You've probably visited housing developments where you can't tell one house from the other—where the condos or McMansions all look alike and even the dogs match— as if one golden Lab got cloned for the whole neighborhood. You may think that what goes on behind closed doors in those almost identical homes is the same, too—all those couples living their happy and materially comfortable lives—and wish you could have a life and marriage just like it. If so, consider this: When the late Princess Diana married Prince Charles and went to live in a castle, it looked for a while like she was living a storybook life, too.

All couples base their marriage blueprints on certain preconceived notions of how marriages are supposed to look or work and how they want *theirs* to look and work—not like their parents', not like the one on *Everybody Loves Raymond*, kind of like the one in *It's a Wonderful Life* but with a little more *9½ Weeks*. Eventually, though, as they live their lives, they begin to realize that they're going to have to put aside aspects of those blueprints—even the parts that were their own original design. After all, how well did you or your partner really know yourselves back when you first got engaged and planned (or didn't plan) your future together? You couldn't know what either of you really wanted or needed as well as you do now. You know yourself better and you know your needs better, and your partner is in the same place. All around, this puts you in a much more informed position to design a marriage that best suits your unique needs as individuals and as a couple, instead of trying to force-fit yourselves into someone else's idea of what marriage should be, which has no relevance to you.

I've met and counseled an incredible variety of couples during twenty years of practice—from the most seemingly traditional to the furthest thing from it and every kind of couple in between. Here are three things I've learned: 1.) Whatever people may think they can tell about a couple or relationship from the outside is usually wrong. 2.) All relationships are more difficult, complicated, and surprising than they appear. 3.) Everyone's looking for love.

A few years ago, I counseled a woman named Eleanor. She was drop-dead gorgeous, had a drop-dead gorgeous husband, two high-achieving kids, and a twenty-five-year marriage that she was the first to admit all her friends envied. She and her husband, Joseph, just seemed so damned happy. Eleanor thought they were, too, until she went to a supermarket one day and was chatted up by the man standing in front of her in the checkout line. Inexplicably, she said, when they left the supermarket, she went back with him to his apartment. They began a torrid affair, and, shortly thereafter, she began divorce proceedings. Her friends were shocked. Her family was shocked. Her husband was shocked, and *she* was shocked. She told me that, for twenty-five years, until she met this man, she had had no idea how unhappy she had been in her life and marriage. For all those years she had been so locked into believing that she had the perfect life, and that she should be happy about it, that she had never thought about whether she really was. She didn't know how she felt or what she wanted, she said. Fortunately, as devastated and shocked as her husband was, he genuinely loved his wife and wanted to save the marriage. Eleanor also cared about her husband and children enough to agree to give the marriage a second chance. That's when they came to me.

In Chapters 8 and 9, I'll discuss ways that you and your husband can get to know yourselves and each other better so you can be better equipped to go after what makes you both happy, however unconventional that may be.

3. Remember, Rome wasn't built in a day. Nor are marital blueprints brought into perfect alignment in a day, or a month, or even a year. You can't rush them. The best advice I can give to this end is this: Never try to tackle more than two discrepancies in blueprints at a time. One at a time is ideal. Don't try to decide where you'll spend all your summer vacations—focus only on this year. Don't try to decide how much you'll put into your IRAs from now on—focus on what you'll deposit this year. That way, there's a sense of continued openness to making other choices about alternative ways of doing things in the future. If one of you wants to buy a new car this year and the other thinks the old car is just fine, work on that issue only and leave other issues aside for the time being. Don't overload yourselves and end up in big fights that overwhelm you both. When a wife hits a husband with too many changes (or vice versa), she defeats her purpose—because no matter how delicately she may think she's broaching these subjects (and there are better and worse ways, as I'll get to soon), her husband will be overwhelmed by her unhappiness (and/or greediness). Then, rather than feel optimistic about working out a glitch, he's likely to be tempted to pick up his paper, pencils, and erasers and walk away. Because, geez, if she's that unhappy (and so oblivious to how hard he's been trying to make her happy), what's the point of a blueprint when the marriage has already been condemned?

Once you've decided what to tackle first—as in, "Okay, the first thing we really need to work on is our finances" or "Sex is our biggest area of difference"—stick with the topic at hand until you figure it out or both of you agree to come back to it at another time.

4. Hang a "Do Not Disturb" sign on the door. When architects are working on an important project, they retreat to their inner office, close the door, and ask their assistants to hold their calls so that they can give the project the attention it deserves. Since you and your husband are unlikely to have an assistant and you have not trained your three-year-old to hold calls, you'll have to choose a quiet and private place to work on your own. No television. No cell phones. No kids needing a ride to the mall. In addition, I'd like to advocate that you not select the bedroom for these conversations—even though it may seem the most private spot in the house, and even though that hour after you both crawl into bed may seem most convenient. I stand by the bedroom—and especially the bed—as being for sleep, relaxation, and sex; not the venue to examine marital conflict. Instead, try taking a ride or a walk together. Or perhaps go to a café or park. (Both food and fresh air can help these kinds of conversations go down a little more smoothly!) After all, couples have much more self-control when they are in a restaurant than in their living room. Not to mention, while women are comfortable talking while doing nothing or anything, men are often more comfortable talking while engaged in an activity. (I'll come back to this point in a moment.)

One very important factor to keep in mind for these conversations: Architects may mainline coffee while working on a big project, but they don't do booze. Nor should couples who are trying to iron out differences in their marriage blueprints. Couples report that many of their worst fights turn out to have been fueled by alcohol. It takes only one sip too many to go from relaxation to trouble. If you can't trust yourself to limit yourself to one glass of wine, it's better to have none.

5. Observe regular work hours. Architects burn the midnight oil when they have a tight design deadline, but even then, when their vision starts to blur, out of respect for the project, they'll call it a night. The same holds for couples who are revising their marriage blueprints. Spouses can talk and work productively for only so long. If they push themselves beyond that point, like architects pushing too hard, they're going to get sloppy and may have to redo their work the next day.

After being married for a certain length of time, many spouses develop a clearer sense of their own and each other's limits and what qualifies as a better or worse time to raise touchy subjects: while out doing Saturday errands, *yes*; when she has just ended a difficult phone conversation with her mother, *no*; when he's trying to watch his cooking show, *no way*. They get to know the natural rhythms of their marriage and, even if they're not aware of it, they begin adapting to these rhythms, working with them instead of against them. They learn how to call time-outs when they sense they're approaching their own breaking point, and their partner learns to honor the warning and be grateful for it. They learn how to read each other's nonverbal signals that a conversation is becoming too painful and pull back even when it goes against the grain. They develop not only a sense of good timing, in other words, but also good discipline and good sense.

If you're not sure what constitutes a good or bad time to initiate "blueprint planning" discussions with your spouse, put it off for a few weeks and observe the natural rhythms of your married life. Ask yourself:

- When is he most receptive to talking in general?
- When do your efforts to initiate a conversation almost always fail?
- Is there anything special going on in his life right now that makes this an especially bad time to talk about relationship problems?
- If you've been married more than a year and don't know the answers to any of these questions already, why is that?

Once you have figured out which are the good talking times, again, start small. Raise an issue. Say something like "You know, honey, I've been thinking we need to review the way we budget." Then ask your husband, "Is this a good time for us to talk or is later better?" If he says later is better, ask him to pick the hour and the place. That way, he won't feel taken by surprise.

6. Prime the pump. Ask men to share memories of pleasant moments they spent with their dads, and many will tell stories about going fishing or building a tree house or working on a car: times when they and their dads may have been talking but they weren't *just* talking—they were talking and *doing*. Men generally prefer to connect with each other by combining talk with some other activity, even if it's a word or two at halftime. That shared external focus makes them feel less on the hot seat and more comfortable opening up. In my years as a therapist, I've found that many husbands would prefer to talk to their wives this way, too. Men like to "do" their way into talking. I once recommended to a husband and wife who were both athletic that they try having their blueprint talks while shooting baskets in their backyard. I know another husband and wife who had some of their best talks while working in their garden. Hiking, having cocoa in a café, or taking that walk in the park I mentioned earlier are also excellent choices.

Nota bene: One of a man's favorite ways of getting in the mood to talk to his wife is by having sex. So the next time your husband wants to jump your bones, instead of huffing to yourself that all he ever wants is sex, remind yourself that sex may be what puts him in a mood to talk. In fact, this (after good sex) is the only time I think it's acceptable to discuss marital blueprints in bed. After good sex, with large amounts of the natural bonding chemical oxytocin floating through their systems, husbands and wives are both likely to speak more gently and lovingly to each other and see their problems in a more hopeful light.

On the other hand, if your husband is the kind who snores after sex, skip this idea.

7. Call a planning meeting to order with style. I hate to support stereotypes, but forgive me, this one is true. There are four words husbands dread hearing above all others: "We need to talk." They know when they hear these words that nothing good can follow. No wife says them when she wants to tell her husband how wonderful he is or when she wants to make love. Husbands know that when a wife speaks those words what she's really saying is, "I'd like your permission to criticize you for being you" or "I'd like you to listen while I tell you how you've let me down" or "I think it's time I told you I'm having an affair with the butcher." It's a phrase that can make a man's blood run cold.

Don't use it. Ever. Instead, open blueprint conversations with warm, neutral, nonthreatening overtures such as:

- "I've been reading this wonderful book and it made me think about us."
- "We've both been so busy lately; it feels like we haven't talked in ages. I've been thinking about how fast Jill is growing. She'll be starting school soon, you know . . ."
- "That was the sweetest thing you did last week when you [fill in the blank with something you genuinely appreciated]. It got me thinking about how lucky I am to be married to you and how much I want us both to do everything we can to stay healthy for each other . . ."

Those are just a few ideas to play with. I'm sure you can come up with other overtures on your own. The point is to think of ways to approach your partner softly and avoid words or phrases that will set off alarm bells and cause him to close off and shut down. But you have to be sincere. No manipulating or trickery, because, trust me, the first time you use a soft approach to lure your husband into a conversation that turns out to be an attack is the last time he'll give you that opening. Which brings me to my next point.

8. Remember that you're building, not tearing down. Your goal in working at drawing up a marital blueprint is to improve the marriage you've created over the years—to repair and renovate your relationship, not demolish it and start over. The best way to do this is to look forward rather than backward (you can't change the past, but you *can* shape the future) and focus on what you *want* from your marriage rather than what you don't want from it. Couples are more successful at making improvements in their relationship when they actually think in terms of *making improvements* rather than in terms of criticizing, complaining, attacking, and bellyaching. Moreover, it is easier to add something positive to their marriage than to eliminate a negative.

And yet, shifting their focus from what is broken or rotted to what they'd like to *improve* in their marriage can be surprisingly difficult for couples to do. When it's clear that attacking and criticizing each other are getting partners nowhere, I'll often say to a husband and wife: "Why don't we try something different. I'd like each of you to tell me what you each want *more of* in your relationship." Frequently, I'll get blank stares, and then the husband and wife will go back to talking about what they *don't* want more of—*I don't want any more of his criticism. I don't want her telling me what to do anymore. I'm tired of him never asking me what I think.*

Sometimes when I repeat my request—"You're both so skilled at knowing what you don't want, but I asked you to tell me what you *do* want"—couples will get angry, as if I don't really care about their problems and don't understand what they're dealing with.

I understand why some couples get so defensive. Asking each other for what they want from each other can be scary. It means making themselves vulnerable to more hurt and rejection, when they're already hurting enough. It's much safer to complain and criticize. Unfortunately, playing it safe (and focusing on the negative) almost never gets spouses what they really want, which is to feel more loved by and connected to their partner.

Samreen and Ken were locked in this kind of defensive, antagonistic mode of interacting when they came to see me a few years ago. They had reached the point where they bickered almost constantly without even realizing it. When I asked them what they each wanted more of from the other, neither could answer. They wrestled with the question through the entire session and couldn't come up with a thing, they were *that* angry at each other. I assured them that this was okay and that couples who are having difficulties can require time to calm down and clear their heads before they can think of an answer. I suggested that they try to monitor their interactions over the next few weeks, and that when one of them said or did even the smallest thing that made the other feel good, they try to note it by saying, "I like that—and I'd like more of that. That makes me feel good."

The breakthrough came three weeks later, when they were in the kitchen cleaning up after dinner. Ken handed Samreen a container of broccoli casserole to put in the fridge. "Thanks," she said, unthinkingly. But Ken caught it. He stopped what he was doing, turned to her and said, "You're welcome." She caught that and looked up. They stood facing each other in silent embarrassment for a moment, and then Samreen said, "I like it when we're nice to each other. It makes me feel good." And Ken said, "Yeah, I like it, too."

That was it—simple as it may seem. That was their breakthrough. They had uncovered one cornerstone of respect and goodwill that still existed between them. Underneath all their hurt and anger, there still existed a natural impulse to be nice to each other. Spotting it and naming it filled them both with hope for their marriage that they hadn't felt in some time. The good feeling between them wasn't completely extinct after all. It was still alive. It could be nurtured and revived. They began building on that. Eventually, they began talking tentatively about what each partner wanted more of in their marriage: affection, passion, respect, appreciation. It was slow going, but as the months went by, they made tremendous progress.

9. Make the blueprint precise! An architect doesn't examine a blueprint for a showcase house, say "It needs more light," and expect his partner to know exactly where he wants more windows installed. Instead, they'll discuss what kind of windows and how big and how many and where. Likewise, it's usually unhelpful for a wife to tell her husband that she wants more affection, and then leave it to him to figure out what "more affection" means. He might genuinely believe that scraping dead bugs off her car windshield is the most affectionate thing he can do, because he knows how much she hates doing it, when what she really wants is for him to put his arm around her when they're watching TV.

Spouses need to be concrete and clear when asking for what they want more of from each other. If you would like your husband to be more affectionate, here are some questions to ask yourself to help you clarify, first to yourself and then to him, exactly what you want.

- What would he be doing or doing more of if he were being more affectionate in the way you desire?
- What else would he be doing?
- Where would he be doing these things?
- For what length of time?
- How many times a week?

Don't overlook those last two questions. A man appreciates being given these specifics. Otherwise he worries that when a wife asks for something, fulfilling her request will be like Chinese water torture. Whatever she wants will go on indefinitely, a never-ending task. He will never be able to let go of her hand or stop hugging her. He worries that when a wife asks for something or says the dreaded words "we need to talk," he'll never see daylight again. Whether you're asking for fifteen minutes of oral sex or two hours of babysitting services, or two hours of oral sex and fifteen minutes of babysitting services, your husband will respond better if you tell him not only what you want him to do but also for how long.

Barbara and Cesar, a couple I counseled recently, had each other going in circles trying to satisfy each other's requests for more affection (hers) and more passion (his) in their marriage, until I walked them through this exercise. Both were surprised at the results. It turned out that despite the things Cesar was doing to show his wife more affection, he wasn't doing the one thing she wanted most. "Cesar," she said, "I like being shown affection in public, not just in private. It means a lot to me. I love it when you hold my hand in public. If you would do that when we're walking down the street, even for ten minutes, it would make me feel great." Cesar smiled. Sure, he said. He could do that. Barbara was pleased and surprised at how doable Cesar's specific request for more display of passion turned out to be. "When we make love," he told her, "you keep your eyes closed. I want you to look at me, at least part of the time. It turns me on." Barbara almost laughed. All those limber displays she'd been coming up with, and this was all he wanted? "Why didn't you say so sooner?" she said, smiling warmly. "If I'd known, I would have opened my eyes long ago. It never crossed my mind."

10. When pushing for revisions, be prepared to accept the consequences of those changes. A client of mine named Rogene complained bitterly when she and her husband, Peter, first came to see me that Peter never confided in her, never told her what he was thinking or feeling. All she ever got were bland statements of fact. "When I ask him how his day went, he'll say, 'We got the report out' or 'Big deadline this week,' and that's it," Rogene complained. "And if I ask him how he's feeling, all he ever says is 'fine' or 'okay,' even when I can see the stress on his face." Peter became increasingly agitated listening to his wife's complaint. Finally he said, "Okay. You want to know what's going on in my head? I'll tell you." He had mouthed off to his boss a couple of weeks ago and had been given an official reprimand, he said. His boss had been avoiding him ever since, and now he was worried about losing his job.

Rogene's eyes widened. "What? You think you're going to get fired? Oh, Peter, no! What did you say? Did you yell? Oh God, tell me you didn't yell! I told you your temper was going to get you in trouble! How many times have I said that? Oh, God, Peter, you can't lose this job! You just can't!"

Peter threw his hands up. "So much for opening up and telling you my worries. I knew you'd freak out."

Now, Rogene may have had good reason to be upset by Peter's revelations, but that's not the point. The point is that she had told her husband that she wanted something from him, and when he gave it to her, she didn't know how to respond to it. In subsequent counseling sessions Rogene came to see that when she said she wanted Peter to share his thoughts and feelings with her, what she really meant was that she wanted him to share the ones that would make her feel good: "You know, you really look beautiful tonight" and "I was just thinking about how much I love you."

Eventually Rogene came to realize that she had unwittingly been clinging to the traditional notion of the man always being the stronger partner. Deep down, the idea of letting Peter be a whole person with weaknesses and strengths frightened her—and Peter had picked up on that and protected her by hiding the less perfect parts of himself. If Rogene genuinely did want her husband to share these less romantic thoughts and worries, she realized, she would have to work on learning how to respond more supportively when he did.

In Chapter 3 I talked about the importance of maintaining a strong foundation of trust in marriage. It was obvious to me from Rogene's reaction that, rightly or wrongly, she didn't trust Peter to be able to handle the problem at his office and, as a result, he now had to deal not only with that problem, but with his anxious wife. Fortunately, because it happened in my office, I was able to be useful and guide Rogene through a repair effort, which she needed to make as soon as possible. In the end what she said was, "Peter, you deserved better from me. I take responsibility for pushing you in a direction you didn't want to go, and I take responsibility for what I just put you through. I have to work on containing myself, and I have to work on learning how to be supportive. I'll do it, and if you think of something that will help, tell me." (*Nota bene*: The person who screws up is responsible for initiating a repair, not the person who has been hurt.) Now they had something to talk about and to work on. Peter was able to name all kinds of ways that Rogene made it hard for him to talk—interrupting, not having faith in him, acting as if she were on the opposing team instead of his team. Rogene listened and some good work was done. Among other things, Rogene realized that she had been cheerleading for a kind of relationship she couldn't handle . . . yet.

Almost all spouses want an ongoing dialogue, true openness and sharing, a vibrant teammate, and a deep sense of working together. However, like many husbands and wives, Peter and Rogene lacked some of the tools they needed to build that kind of marriage. The responsibility for their difficulties wasn't only Rogene's. Peter could have raised the issue of being shut out from expressing his real feelings because of her anxiety sooner than he did, too. He could have found ways to get the ball rolling, but he didn't because he didn't know how, because he was tired, because he didn't have faith it would work, and so on.

Without the right relationship tools, these kinds of misunderstandings, silences, and overreactions happen often. Now that you know the fundamentals for forming a master plan for marriage renovations and repairs, I'll turn to the matter of the tools couples need to have at hand, and which they need to toss, before embarking on these improvement projects.

CHAPTER 5

The Five Essential Tools Do-It-Yourselfers Need for Renovation and Repair

Blueprint in place, you and your spouse now have a current, shared plan to expand, renovate, or repair your relationship. As any contractor would do when preparing for a home construction project, the next step is to assemble the necessary tools for the job.

First, it helps to be reminded again that, with homes and spouses, building conditions often will be less than perfect. During any renovation, a house will have leaks and cracks and funky smells and mold. The relationship equivalent is more stress, more bitterness, more outbursts. Like a bathroom in mid-repair, things will often get worse before they get better. But, rest assured, they *will* get better.

The Value of Always Having a Well-Stocked Toolbox Handy: A Tale of Two Marriages

It was the best of times and it was the worst of times for Meg and her sister, Marcy. While growing up, their father, a minor TV personality, had numerous affairs that he didn't even try to hide. Their mother, a stay-at-home mom, put up with it, but suffered loudly. Both sisters felt much pain and humiliation growing up in a home with this parental dynamic.

Fast-forward twenty years, and Meg and Marcy are married to men more faithful than their father, yet they are both quite sensitive on the subject of infidelity. Let's join them at two separate holiday parties where they face similarly skeevy situations.

Meg and her husband, Tim, attended a party at the home of one his colleagues. She didn't know anyone there, and she'd always felt that neither high school reunions nor office Christmas parties should be foisted on the spouse. Still, she was having a nice enough time until she glanced up from the buffet table and saw Tim break a piece of mistletoe off a wreath and dangle it over his own head with a goofy grin on his face. Two of his young female colleagues laughed as they walked past and gave him a quick peck on the cheek. That was all it took. Meg walked into another room, sat down near the fireplace, and avoided Tim for the rest of the night. But the minute they were alone in the car, she exploded: "How could you *do* that to me? How could you let those women kiss you? You are brutal, just brutal. I am so humiliated that you have so little respect for me that you would behave that way right in front of my face." Feeling completely suckerpunched, Tim drove home in silence, choking on his own anger and worried now that everyone else also thought he had acted like an ass.

That same week, Marcy and her husband, Rich, were at a holiday party at the home of a neighbor. Shortly after arriving, when Marcy walked into the other room to sit with friends, a woman who'd just moved in down the street started hitting on Rich, hanging on his arm, laughing and displaying her cleavage like *Married with Children*'s Peggy Bundy. After a few minutes, Marcy walked back into the room. Rich did not appear to be suffering. Seeing them, she walked over, took her husband's arm, and said softly, with a smile, "I'm getting that family feeling."

The phrase "family feeling" was a code they'd agreed upon for when either one of them felt anxious about something while they were out in public. They had picked the phrase because they both had old family injuries that flared up under certain circumstances. In Rich's case, it often had to do with feeling ignored, as he had been in his family of origin. On this night, it was Marcy's code for signaling to Rich that the kind of attention he was paying to another woman upset her. "You think I need to watch out?" Rich asked Marcy, giving her a wink. "If you want to get lucky with *me* tonight you will," she answered. He laughed, put a hand on her back, and guided her toward the bar. "Let's get some wine." And, that settled, Rich and Marcy went on with the party.

When faced with an emotional challenge, each of these two couples handled the situation very differently, leading to very different outcomes—not because the challenges of each situation were all that different, but because one of the couples (Marcy and Rich) had assembled a toolbox for such occasions. They'd been through this before (haven't we all?), and together, they'd agreed on a plan for the next time. Meg and Tim were aware of their hot spots, too. However, they hadn't figured out how to stop having the same fight over and over again, for years: a fight that a few conversations could have obviated once and for all.

With houses, you know that the quality of any improvements you make depends on the quality of your (or your contractor's) tools, skills, and approach. The above example shows how the quality of your tools, skills, and approach is equally important for making improvements in your marriage.

Having read this far, you've already completed four important steps:

1. You've faced the fact that your marriage needs to be improved.
2. You've reappraised your relationship and decided that even though it's not perfect, it has value and is worth working on.
3. You've done a quick inspection of the foundation of trust in your marriage to check for damage and do quick repairs.
4. You've examined your marriage blueprint and have a pretty good idea of what improvements you'd like to make to your relationship, what you want your life together to look like in the future, and which repair you should tackle first.

So far, what you've done is think, frame, gather information, imagine, understand, and integrate. Now, as we get ready to roll up our sleeves and begin the grunt work, the final step in the preparation process involves a trip to an emotional Home Depot of sorts, to gather the tools (and skills) that are essential for quality construction and repair. Then, back at home, you'll toss the ones that create more problems than they fix.

TOOL #1: A Cool Head

Panicky Guesswork Only Leads to Disasters

Anyone who has ever stood on a chair holding the frosted-glass globe of a ceiling light fixture overhead with one hand, while trying to tighten the tiny little screws that are supposed to hold it in place in a metal rim with the other, knows that even the simplest of household repairs is more taxing than homeowners expect. Relationship repairs generally are more taxing than you'd expect, too. Both require keeping a cool head when the chair starts to tip or the balance of how you and your spouse are getting along starts to tip. Here are three rules everyone should follow when faced with home or relationship repairs to avoid making them any harder or more taxing than they have to be.

Don't panic. Bad feelings and bad moods don't mean "this marriage is condemned" any more than bad leaks and bad doorknobs mean that a house is condemned. However, when making home repairs, there is one emotion that has been known to lead otherwise sane individuals to whip out the sledgehammer when a well-placed squirt of WD-40 would have done the trick. It is the same emotion that, when unleashed in a marriage, frequently causes just as much of an overreaction and is just as dangerous: panic. Panic makes us say and do a range of misguided things, from breaking down a door to yelling "I want a divorce!"

In all the work I do and in every intervention I use, my biggest challenge, my most difficult adventure with a struggling couple, is to help spouses not to panic when things get rough. When relationship security and happiness feel threatened, even by the smallest thing, spouses' reactions can be similar to being stuck in an elevator or being a passenger on a very bumpy plane ride: Their adrenaline shoots up, their heart rate increases, the "fight or flight" syndrome kicks into gear. On a plane, though, the flight attendant is well trained to calm people, and, in an elevator, people can reach for the emergency phone or button. When a relationship hits a bump or gets stuck and partners panic, they have no one to prevent them from acting on their panicky impulses. In that state, couples often do things they later regret. They behave irrationally. That's the definition of panic.

So what stops panic? Sheer force of will. We'll address that later, but for now, think *discipline*, and keep reading.

Keep in mind that, sometimes, a leak is just a leak. If the stovetop burners on a gas range don't light, it makes sense to check the pilot light before calling the gas company. And if your AC unit stops working, you'd want to make sure it's plugged in before going out and buying a new one. The same reasoning goes for relationships—problems that at first seem dire often aren't. Sometimes spouses snap at each other or hurt each other simply because they are in a bad mood, or are having a bad day—no other, deeper reason than that. And while it's not fair that the other partner has to bear the brunt of that, sometimes the best move is to suck it up and say, "You must be tired. Why don't you relax while I start dinner?" Again, sheer force of will!

And on those when days you can't do that—because you had a hard day, too, or because your spouse has had 643 hard days in a row—the next best thing to do is to say one simple word: "ouch"! When you say "ouch," you make it clear that you've been hurt, but it is not a blaming statement, so it is unlikely to agitate your partner further. Simple, I know, but it gets the message across very effectively.

If you say "ouch," and your partner says, "What's that supposed to mean?" do the next best thing—*duck*. He's looking for a fight (we've all been guilty of this from time to time), and you've got about ten seconds to figure out the wisest course of action. Sometimes, that means saying you're sorry when you didn't do anything. Or you might say, "I'm going to run to the corner store. I forgot to pick up something. Do you need anything?" and give your partner a chance to cool off. In this situation, since your partner doesn't seem to know he is cranky and testy, this would not be an opportune time to try to set him straight.

Don't do today what you can put off until after you calm down. If you find yourself overwhelmed during a relationship-repair job, if you know your self-control is such that if you open your mouth at a particular moment, you are guaranteed to make things worse, *just say so*.

Say: We need to deal with this, but I know that right now, anything I say will only make it worse. Let's both sleep on it and try again tomorrow.

Say: Believe me, I wish I could do better right now, but I'm too upset. I don't want to hurt you or hurt myself. Let me get better control first.

Say: I'm going to walk around the block. You can't count on me right now to be of any help, but after I cool off, we'll figure it out.

Take the high road. Later, you'll be glad you didn't reach for that hammer and start trying to pound your point home. You've likely been in a relationship long enough to know just how much damage can be done in a nanosecond.

TOOL #2: Humility

You're a Novice, and All Novices Make Mistakes—the Best Ones Learn from Them

My friend Tom is a professional carpenter. A few years ago, he decided he wanted to add to his repertoire of skills, so he apprenticed with a banister maker to learn how to make beautiful curvy banisters.

After being taught the basics of how to make a banister, he approached the piece of wood three times, and each time, he got the curve wrong. First the curve started too soon, then it started too late, then too soon again. After the third try, he put down his tools loudly and sat in a chair and sulked, at which point his boss came over and said, "Poor Tom. You tried three whole times to do what I've spent twenty years of my life trying to perfect, and you didn't get it right. Maybe you should consider training to be an X-ray technician."

The point: Some of the most desired skills in any profession require twenty tries, thirty tries, forty to one hundred tries to master and perfect. And mastering new ways of relating to each other in a relationship can require just as many tries to get right, and deserve no less.

Everyone has (or should have) stages of relationship apprenticeship. There are many ways to learn: reading a relationship book, watching a videotape, trial and error, apprenticing to a master. All, however, involve one essential three-step cycle: 1) making mistakes; 2) learning from those mistakes or having them pointed out and corrected (so you can go on to make new ones); and 3) trying the task again and again and again.

Regardless of whether you learned French faster than anyone in your class, or whether you were the only one not to fall down when learning how to ski, relationships may or may not come easily to you. So, consider a visit to the land of humility—the place where you are not only willing, but have an actual desire to know: "What am I doing wrong and how can I do it better?"

Ask yourself: What makes me impossible to live with?

Remember that list you made back in Chapter 2 of all the reasons you detest your partner from time to time? Long list? Probably. Want to add to it? Go ahead. Then let's make a similar list about yourself.

Often, when couples come to my office, one partner has assumed the role of the aggrieved spouse, and the other has taken on the role of guilty partner. That's why I always ask both partners to tell me why *they* are impossible to live with. This tells me how much the spouse playing the aggrieved partner is wedded to that role: "What makes *me* impossible to live with? Excuse me, but that's not why we're here. We're here because *he* . . ." When one or both partners won't answer this question and insist they are clueless about any part of the problem they might own, I know that helping them improve their relationship is going to take time. *Both* partners contribute to what is going right in their marriage, and *both* partners contribute to what isn't working. Without that basic assumption, repairs take longer. The truth is, if a person refuses to see his or her contribution to the problem, I can't be of much help.

On the chance that you need help identifying your own negative habits and behaviors, here are some of the most common relationship crimes spouses are guilty of:

- You are unable to see your own flaws.
- You would rather focus on collecting and counting hurts and injustices than examining your own behavior. You don't like looking inward and try to avoid it.
- You're angry at your husband about something, but you're afraid to talk about it with him because you're not sure how he'll react or how your marriage will be affected if you do. So you take it out on him by criticizing him in countless other ways.
- You know that making your husband feel guilty is a way of getting attention from him and you do it for that reason.
- You can't drop an argument until your husband admits he's wrong and says he's sorry.

- You have to get the last word.
- You make jokes at your husband's expense in front of other people.
- You say hurtful things when you feel wronged or attacked.
- You tease him about things you know he's sensitive about.

The point of this exercise isn't to beat yourself up about past sins, but simply to become more aware of them, so you can begin to see the ways in which you are contributing to whatever problems you are experiencing. You have to know what you're repairing in order to repair it.

Whatever relationship crimes you're guilty of committing, STOP!

Let's say you're beginning to consider that you *do* tease your partner about things you shouldn't. Try this: Stop doing it. Don't tell him you're going to stop. Don't call attention to the fact that you have stopped. Just do it, and watch to determine whether, over time, you feel a slight easing of tension between you. In my experience, that small, one-sided repair effort can have a notably positive effect on a marriage.

TOOL #3: Curiosity

Dedicated Do-It-Yourselfers Love Figuring Out How (and Why) Things Work

When couples are hurt and angry, they can misread each other's intentions and distort each other's actions and words. Spouses see the worst in each other, and this *brings out* the worst in them.

Unable to see or hear themselves, they become defensive and hostile, flinging insults and accusations every which way.

Jumping to hostile conclusions and acting out in moments of defensiveness or frustration when a relationship-repair job doesn't go well does not help to get the job done. It's the equivalent of junking a lawn mower that won't start after the gas tank is refilled without first checking to see if the blades are clogged with grass. Much more useful is the reaction to which good do-it-yourselfers switch, a state of mind that reflects a certain relish for information gathering and puzzle solving. Instead of getting angry when things hit a snag, they get *curious* about what the true cause of the problem is: "I seem to be missing something here. I'm not sure what it is yet, but I'll figure it out—and learn a thing or two in the process."

Curiosity may have killed the cat, but it can save your marriage. Here are two examples drawn from my practice of what can happen when spouses respond defensively to something their mate says, and how differently events might unfold if they stay open and curious.

Situation # 1: Hank came home one evening from his job as a public affairs officer for a phone company and told his wife, Ursula, "I'm thinking about going back to school."

Defensive Response: "Are you crazy?" Ursula snapped. "We can't live on my salary alone." "Are *you* crazy?" Hank snapped back. "Do you want me to stay in a job I hate and be miserable the rest of my life?"

Curiosity Response: If Ursula had asked, "Really? What started you thinking about that?" Hank would have told her, as he did later in my office, that he had found out that his company pays tuition benefits for continuing education and that he hadn't intended to quit his job at all. He was thinking of going to night school for his master's degree. The company would pay for his courses, and he'd get a promotion when he was through.

Situation # 2: Sandra announced to her husband, Ed, "I have to stop driving Lilly to school every morning. I'm getting into the office late too often, and my boss is starting to grumble."

Defensive Response: "Well, I certainly hope you don't think *I'm* going to do it," Ed said. "My drive is just as long, and her school isn't even on the way." "Thanks a lot," Sandra said acidly. "That is so like you. Always looking out for number one."

Curiosity Response: If Ed had said, "Gee, I'm sorry, honey. What do you think we should do?" Sandra could have explained, as she did in my office, that Lilly had been asking to ride the school bus to school like all her friends did, and Sandra thought that might be the perfect solution. It would mean having to get Lilly out the door earlier, which would get Sandra on the road to work earlier, too.

Like keeping a cool head, exercising curiosity during trying times is an act of will, one that can require a lot of practice. Couples who do, however, are often pleasantly surprised to find that, after a while, the information-gathering mode of interacting starts to feel more natural and eventually becomes as automatic as hostility and defensiveness were before. There are four main ways to develop and strengthen this "curiosity response."

1. Practice saying "Tell me more." This, or some version of it ("Tell me what you're thinking" or "Keep talking, I'm listening"), may be the most common words spoken in a psychotherapy treatment office. I often say some version of it twenty times before I really understand a situation. I offer these same three little magic words to you so that, if your husband says something—anything—

that upsets you, you will resist all forms of defensive, angry, or critical response. Your tone, manner, and gestures must be sincere when delivering them. (No sarcastic sniper attacks such as, "Oh, really? Tell me more, why don't you?" with a smirk on your face and your arms crossed over your chest.) "Tell me more," done right, conveys that you are listening rather than waiting to pounce, and that you're ready to give him all the time he needs to explain himself. "Tell me more" is an invitation to have a safe conversation in a safe place.

2. Clarify as you go. If your spouse's comment rattles or inflames you, do not assume you heard him correctly. In fact, assume you didn't, and ask him to repeat himself. Say: "Would you mind repeating that? I want to make sure I understand." Or, as many marriage counselors recommend, you can always repeat his words and ask him if you are getting it right.

A colleague of mine told me a story recently that perfectly illustrates how important seeking clarification can be. She and her husband had gone on one of their occasional one-night getaways to their favorite B&B and were lying in bed after making love. Filled with tender feelings toward him and wishing she could be a more perfect and loving wife than she knew she sometimes was, she said to him softly, "Sometimes I think I don't love you well enough." Her husband smarted at that and asked, "What do you mean?" It wasn't until she saw his worried expression that she realized that what she was trying to say hadn't come out right at all. "He heard, 'Sometimes I don't think I love you *enough*,'" she told me, looking stricken. "Can you imagine? And I wouldn't have known if he hadn't said something." It's so easy for spouses to misunderstand each other and it takes so little effort to avoid it that I urge all couples to make the effort to clarify almost everything said in every conversation they have, even when they're sure they understand each other, because it's often when they're most sure they do that they actually don't. Making this extra effort helps them avoid so many unnecessary misunderstandings that it's worth whatever extra time it may involve, even if this means adding twenty minutes to the conversation and sounding like Abbott and Costello.

3. Be an emotional Sherlock and keep asking questions. Like an emotional detective, until you have heard everything your husband has to say and gathered all the information, you won't know if there was even a crime committed, so don't jump to conclusions. In addition, like Sherlock, be slow, methodical, and patient, or you may miss something important. If your partner is long-winded or is one of those folks who dances around a point, resist the urge to finish his sentences or to interrupt. And avoid offering unasked-for feedback, even if you have to clamp a hand over your mouth to keep from doing it. Just keep asking questions: "Why does that idea appeal to you?" "What started you thinking about that?" "How do you think we would make that work?" "How would our life change?" And always: "Is there more?" "Is there more?" "Is there more?"

4. Limit your early response. Active listening is hard work. Expect to sweat and possibly even vibrate. When you reach the point where you "get it," thank him for telling you and say, "This is a lot to take in. So give me some time to process what you've said. Then we'll talk more." This goes whether your partner wants another child, another chance, or another face lift. It's always wise to let yourself process a conversation overnight, and then consider asking for another information-gathering conversation the following day or week. At this next conversation, you can make sure you still understand, and then offer some preliminary thoughts: "This could be great" or "This could be hard on me" or "I'm not sure what our lives would be like." But I caution against plunging right into trying to resolve a problem or come to an agreement quickly, because big decisions shouldn't be impulsive. People should always sleep on them at least one night and discuss them more than once. For now, simply repeat "You've given me a lot to think about. How about we let things mulch for a week and talk again?" You're both going to be tired at this point, and you will both have a lot to think over. Throwing in a little hug at the end is always a nice idea, too.

TOOL #4: Empathy

Gifted Do-It-Yourselfers Don't Just Have Good Skills— They Have Good Instincts and a Real Affinity for the Work

Almost anyone can be taught how to hammer a nail effectively. I've even watched horses do it on Animal Planet. It takes more than that, though, to become a fine carpenter or furniture maker. A great furniture maker has that "something" that can't really be taught, only cultivated: a certain natural talent and affinity for the work; a special instinct or intuition.

Almost anyone can get married, too. I've even watched bulldogs do it on Animal Planet, with a pug as ring bearer—but it takes more to excel at marriage than simply taking a vow and tossing a bouquet. Great spouses also cultivate a certain sensitivity, caring, and concern for each other. Great spouses develop and make full use of their empathy.

All spouses occasionally lose it, blow up, and curse, but spouses who experience genuine empathy for each other are much less likely

to strike out in anger, because they are so keenly aware of their partner's feelings that the thought of inflicting intentional hurt becomes
painful. Where empathy grows, intimacy grows with it, along with
understanding. And as a result, couples who cultivate empathy have
many fewer fights.

Real empathy cannot happen without deep listening. In his
bestselling book *The Road Less Traveled*, the late psychiatrist
M. Scott Peck called this type of listening simply "paying attention."
Real empathy requires that you pay attention to your spouse in
new ways, becoming attuned to how he experiences the world and
putting his welfare on a plane with your own (and vice versa, of
course).

Cultivating empathy takes active effort and stretching—in part
because, in many ways, we humans are very self-absorbed, and
are most interested in what pertains to us. (Ever notice how you
can hear someone speaking your name even across a crowded
room?) We are also quite adept at filtering out what we don't want
to hear and what has little to do with our own well-being—often
without knowing we're doing it. Every day in my practice, I see
spouses who believe they pay genuine attention to each other, but
don't know each other as well as they think, or as well as they'd like.
Two small examples from my practice: There was the time that
Jared returned from a business trip to France with a pound of Brie
cheese for Milana because he remembered that she loved all things
French—forgetting, to her dismay, that she was lactose intolerant.
And there was the time Kayla accepted an invitation for her and
Brad to spend a weekend at the country home of a couple they had
met at a party, knowing how much he had been wanting to get
away but failing to notice how much he disliked this other husband.
In and out of my practice, it is a rare day when I run into a couple

who couldn't benefit from learning how to pay more and closer attention.

In sum, an empathetic partner:

- Understands and is sensitive to how her spouse views the world
- Knows and is gentle with his secret fears, hurts, and insecurities, as well as his unspoken hopes and dreams
- Knows how to read and interpret nonverbal cues to what he's feeling and thinking
- Is aware of how her words and behaviors may affect him
- Tries to avoid hurting him; holds his feelings as gently as a mother holds a baby
- Makes room for the expression of all kinds of feelings without repercussions

Women are luckier than men when it comes to empathy. It is built into us from youth in anticipation of our becoming future moms. We hear the baby cry before she opens her mouth. When our best friend says she's fine, we know she's lying. We're tuned in. However, when we are in a rut with our spouse, we often tune out. Here are a few ways to turn your internal radio dial a little closer to his station.

1. Study how he gives himself away. Observe your partner's facial expressions, speech patterns, gestures, and posture when you know he's trying to hide something. For example, while he's talking to a cousin at a family gathering and you hear him say, "Yeah, things are fine, no news is good news, I guess," when the reality is that he's on the verge of being downsized, or you know he really dislikes talking to this cousin, or you've just found out you're pregnant with your first child but you've both agreed not to tell anyone yet.

• When Larry's wife began studying him more closely, she discovered that he taps his foot incessantly when he's anxious. She now knows that, sometimes, she can trust what he's doing with that foot to tell her what he's feeling more than she can trust what he says.

• When Suzanne's husband started studying her, he began to realize that she wasn't really the constantly sunny personality she tried to present herself as being—that she was actually quite sensitive to other people's slights and comments and that the more they hurt her, the harder she smiled.

• When Harry's wife began studying him, she noticed that when he was worried about something but didn't want her to know it, he would insist he was fine, give her a kiss and a squeeze, then walk around the house, clearing his throat.

2. **Respect his feelings, even when you don't share them.** I talked earlier about how to respond with curiosity rather than defensiveness when your husband says something that upsets you. The next step—the more difficult one—is to encourage him to tell you not just what he's thinking but also how he's *feeling*, and to be able to accept his feelings although they may upset you, even when you really wish he didn't feel the way he does.

Your first impulse at times like these may be to block out his feelings or argue with him: "Oh, you don't really mean that." "You know perfectly well . . ." "It can't really be that bad." Even though we want very much to be fair and let our spouse have an equal number of mini breakdowns, women often find it very hard when men's mini breakdowns actually happen. Smart women let men get it all out, though. They listen hard, and they learn. They encourage their spouse to open up by making "tell me more" statements.

3. Never assume. The flip side of resisting the impulse to squelch or dismiss your husband's feelings just because you don't share them (or don't like them) is resisting the impulse to assume that because *you* think or feel something, he does, too. You might be right. But you could be wrong. Men tend to be guiltier of failing to distinguish their desires from their partner's in certain arenas: gift-giving, for example. A male client once told me that he wanted to do something special for his wife on Valentine's Day, so he was making her a tape of all his favorite golden oldies. When I asked what made him think of it, he said, "Well, I love these songs so she will, too." (He actually said that.) I know another man who got his wife a German shepherd puppy as a surprise fiftieth-birthday present because he thought it would be good for her to have a puppy now that the kids were out of the house . . . and because he liked German shepherds.

Women don't necessarily make these mistakes, but they make their own. They may assume, for example, that because a situation makes them anxious, it makes their husband anxious, too—when, in fact, it may not. Or they may assume that because they like to talk out all their worries, their spouse does, too, when all he really wants is some quiet time to sort through his thoughts.

Many spouses believe life would be easier if they agreed on everything, because they think this would mean a more secure life, but life doesn't always work that way. And it would be pretty boring if it did. Couples often prefer to think that if they agreed on everything, they'd never fight. True. However, they'd probably also never have a whole lot of fun (or great sex). It's that little tension that makes a kite fly and a couple soar. The truth is, spouses who embrace differences build a marriage that is roomier and more comfortable for them both. We learn and grow and thrive from the many ways we cooperate and accommodate such differences, not only from the ways we agree.

Rather than act on assumptions of sameness, try testing various assumptions you may have about your husband's thoughts and feelings by asking questions such as:

- "You sound worried. Are you?"
- "That sounds pretty confusing to me. Is it confusing to you?"
- "I know what I'd think if someone said that to me. What do you make of it?"

TOOL #5: Humor

Keep That Silicone Spray Handy! Sometimes, When Things Get Stuck, a Quick Squirt Is All You Need

Benny and Brenda told me that they once visited a marriage counselor who suggested that the next time they started fighting they should stop speaking English and start making excited chimpanzee noises, like Tarzan's Cheetah: "Ooh-ooh-ooh-ooh-*ooh*!" They never went back. What kind of advice was that? But then, about two months later, in the middle of a nasty fight and out of words, Benny began pounding his chest and making excited ape noises—ooh-ooh-ooh-ooh-*ooh*!—and, before they knew it, they were both beating their chests and laughing.

Ellen told me that when she and Jim start edging up to a dangerous fever pitch, he'll sometimes put on an exaggerated, comical, hangdog look that invariably cracks her up. "I can't stay angry when he does that," she said. "Sometimes, if I'm really worked up, I'll try to get angry about not being able to stay angry, but it's hopeless. When I think of how many horrible fights have been averted that way, I want to kiss him."

Spouses should study what each does, intentionally or unintentionally, that makes the other laugh—which quirky expressions, private jokes, and silly ploys seem almost magically effective at cutting through accumulated anger and frustration and redirecting that energy toward laughter and feeling good again. I never cease to be surprised at how close screaming and laughing can be to each other, or how idiosyncratic they are to each couple. What's hilarious to one husband and wife—sticking out their tongues at each other and flapping their arms—makes other couples roll their eyes. I have seen everything from breaking into baby talk to conducting a fight in pig Latin work. Only the two of you know the ridiculous things you do behind closed doors. As Joann Woodward said about Paul Newman (though it may be hard to believe), "Sexiness wears thin after a while and beauty fades, but to be married to a man who makes you laugh every day, ah, now that's a real treat."

CHAPTER 6

The Five Tools and Supplies That Do More Damage Than Good

ow that you know about the five tools that are *essential* for improving a relationship, in this chapter I'll run through a list of five types of tools that need to be banished from your toolbox—tools that many couples automatically reach for when trying to make marriage repairs and which are absolutely the *wrong* tools for the job.

Many of these automatic behaviors and responses are so deeply ingrained that partners may not even realize they're resorting to them, much less how often they do or how counterproductive they are. Spouses may be aware that something's not working, but they don't know what or why. They often can find only one conclusion to draw: The marriage was a mistake. They're with the wrong person. Might as well admit it and call it quits.

In the majority of these cases, however, the spouses didn't pick the wrong partner or make a bad marriage. Instead, they picked up the wrong tools for repair work—tools that only make their problems worse. It's like trying to remove a smudge of dirt on a fine were both acting out their feelings (what kids do) instead of putting their feelings into words (what adults do). Acting out is what happens when emotions run high and children (because they're children) and poorly behaved adults (because they're behaving like children) claim to be justified in punishing you with what they *do* instead of talking with you about how they *feel*. (For example: "It really upsets me when you yell at me," or "I don't like it when you buy tickets to a play without asking whether I want to see it.")

Fortunately, in these two cases, the worst harm done was a spoiled evening and a strain on the budget. Bad enough, but I've seen worse. One couple I counseled named George and Loretta got into a heated argument on their way home from a movie, and the angrier George got, the faster he drove. When Loretta begged him to slow down, he hit the gas pedal even harder. Loretta was terrified. They made it home, and George apologized to Loretta later, but with qualifications. He said, "You get me so mad . . ."—as if that might justify his behavior. But Loretta was badly shaken, and rightly so. Adult temper tantrums of this type are a far more dangerous way of acting out.

All spouses bring some childish behaviors into marriage. Many of these behaviors are harmless, some can even be endearing: She likes to lie on the couch wrapped in a blanket and eat vanilla ice cream when she has a fever, just as she did when she was a little girl. He loves flying kites on the beach in winter, just as he did as a boy. She just can't let go of that teddy bear even though she's thirty-two. But some of these behaviors are not the least endearing. They're counterproductive at best and destructive at worst. They're deeply ingrained behaviors that are called upon so automatically and can pass so quickly that the spouse who indulges in them may have real trouble seeing them as a problem: "So I bought a dress. Big deal." "Okay, so I was speeding. But I've never had an accident in my life."

What's a wife or husband to do when asked to play reasonable grown-up to an irrational spouse who takes on the role of bully or brat? It isn't fair to ask any spouse to put up with this. And you can't send your husband to detention. So, what choices do you have? You certainly don't want to sink to the same level, although, unfortunately, this happens often enough. And telling your partner to "grow up" is not usually very helpful.

A suggestion: At a time when the two of you are relaxed and not fighting, make a pact with your husband. Tell him that you realize that both of you can hit below the belt sometimes, and you know how bad you both feel afterward. Suggest that the next time he notices you beginning to resort to bad (childish) behavior, he should nip it in the bud with a signal that the two of you agree on. And you'd like to do the same. When he takes the low road, you want to use the same signal for him—something that says "You're doing it again"—rather than get angry or make a counterattack. Couples who agree on a funny signal—maybe one of you can slap your bum or stick out your tongue—seem to do much better. Of course, just as when you remodel your home, you should treat the worst cases and the worst places first. No resorting to this signal every time one of you does the littlest thing the other doesn't like.

Whatever signal the two of you come up with, chances are, it will last only a few years and then you'll have to make up something new, because the more you use it, the less effective it becomes. You also have to agree that neither of you gets to argue with a signal—it has to be like a flag down on a football field. Play stops. If the spouse who gets flagged doesn't know why, he or she can initiate an information-gathering session like the one described in Chapter 5, but questions only. No arguing with what the other partner says. If the offending spouse *does* know what foul was committed, he or she is responsible for admitting it and initiating a repair, as described in Chapter 4.

2. The Two-Ton Sledgehammer: Brutal Honesty

I once read a magazine article about a recently wed celebrity couple who said that one of the reasons they thought their marriage was so solid was that they told each other everything, no holding back. *Really?* I thought. *Everything?* These two people aren't together anymore, and the truth is it doesn't surprise me—not because they're celebrities (though fame presents its own risks), but because I don't know of any relationship that could withstand the constant assault of total honesty.

Spouses can say incredibly hurtful things to each other under the guise of "being honest." I recall a couple named Harry and Jessica who came to see me about a year after the birth of their second child. During their fourth session, Jessica finally found the courage to confess that one of the reasons she had wanted counseling was because she seemed to be more interested in sex lately than Harry was, and she was concerned about that, because it isn't the way things used to be. "Well," Harry said, shifting and frowning, "it bothers me that you haven't lost those twenty pounds you gained when you were pregnant." Jessica stared at him in shock for a moment. "You really are a jerk," she said finally and burst into tears. Harry shifted and frowned again. "Look, I'm only being honest," he said, sounding annoyed. "You want me to be honest, don't you?"

"Harry," I said calmly as Jessica continued to cry, "you need to learn the difference between honesty and cruelty." That was a bit of a sledgehammer blow itself, I realized from his startled reaction.

"Honesty is important, you're correct about that," I said more gently. "But honesty without compassion is rightly called something else: brutality."

Now you see why it's so important for spouses to develop empathy for each other. Empathy (the ability and desire to understand and relate to someone else's feelings) and compassion (a deep awareness of another person's pain and a desire to relieve it) are inextricably intertwined. If Harry had more empathy for Jessica, he would have known from the self-deprecating comments she made about her weight and the way she always frowned when she looked at herself in a full-length mirror that she was painfully aware that she was still carrying extra pounds. If he had more compassion for her, he would have known how badly she already felt about that and how deeply his comment would wound her—and he wouldn't have made it.

Honesty *is* important in marriage, no question. The challenge is for spouses to figure out how to communicate feelings, desires, needs, and dissatisfactions in ways that affirm their mutual belief that they are both safe in their marriage—that they can rely on their partner to protect their feelings and be gentle. Spouses who do this are essentially always strengthening the foundation of trust in their marriage. Spouses who don't, and who continually trample on each other's feelings, instead take a sledgehammer not just to every room in the house of their marriage but to its very foundation.

There are numerous methods to convey potentially hurtful messages in ways that don't hurt, or at least don't hurt as much. Here are three things to keep in mind when trying to shape these messages:

1. Be clear about what you want from your partner. Not what you *don't* want—what you *do* want. Be able to state it to yourself in

positive rather than negative terms. That may sound easy, but as I described in Chapter 4, many couples find this hard to do, at least at first. Stay with this step until you've mastered it. Remember that when you feel an urge to criticize or attack your partner, it's often a sign that you're upset because you're not getting something you want. Figure out what that is and you're halfway home.

2. Now think about how you can express your desire in words that keep the focus on *you* and that avoid judging your spouse. The safest way to do this is to talk in terms of "I" rather than "you." To help you remember this tip, think of the "I" of the storm.

3. *Speak* about yourself, but *think* about your partner. Give careful thought to how your words are likely to affect your spouse *before* you utter them, because if what you say does hurt your partner, no matter how much you didn't mean for that to happen, the damage is done.

Here are a few examples of hurtful versus kind ways to express the same truth.

Brutal: Some husband and father you are. You'd rather hang out with your buddies than spend time with me and the kids.

Honest: I miss you, and I think the kids do, too. I'd love for us to spend a day together, just having fun as a family.

Brutal: Your mother is such a witch. No wonder you're so screwed up.

Honest: You deserve extra credit for being so patient with your mom.

Brutal: I hate that shirt. It makes you look like a troll.
Honest: I love the way you look in your gray shirt. Would you mind wearing that one for me?

Brutal: That is the most asinine thing I've ever heard in my life.
Honest: I disagree.

Sometimes, of course, spouses can try every which way from Sunday to communicate a difficult message gently, and their partner still won't get it. As described in Chapter 5, people are much more skilled than they realize at filtering out messages they don't want to hear. In some situations, when a message needs to be communicated urgently, there may also be no time for a spouse to ponder a delicate way to say it. But there is always time to warn a partner that a painful truth is coming his way. The rule, always, is to try to be gentle:

- "I have to say something that I know you're not going to want to hear."
- "There's good news and there's bad news."
- "I've been trying to tell you this for weeks, but I don't feel like I've been able to reach you, so . . ."

Finally, think very carefully about expressing desires your partner wishes he could satisfy but can't (like wishing he were as handsome as Antonio Banderas or as rich as Bill Gates). No matter how much you tell yourself you're expressing these desires as "I" statements that don't reflect on him—"I wish I could just quit my job and stay home"—the reality is you're slipping a screwdriver between his ribs. Your intentions don't matter when your spouse is reeling from what you've just said. Couples who want to protect each other's feelings have faced the facts: Some things should just never be said at all. "I wish you had a bigger penis" is one. "Your weight gain turns me off" is another. Harry could have waited until Jessica said something about her weight and responded with something supportive and loving: "Let's take a walk after dinner instead of watching television" or "You feel bad about the weight you've gained? How can we work together to make you feel better?" Warning, though: If you try this approach, and it looks like your spouse is never going to get around to mentioning the flaw you're so ready to help him improve on, it could mean he sees no need to make any improvements, and you may have to make peace with accepting him as he is. I'll talk more about the art of accepting in Chapter 11.

3. Chisels and Awls: Nagging

If you've ever been nagged by someone about something—and who hasn't?—you might enjoy knowing where the word "nag" comes from. Apparently, it derives from the Old Norse and Old English words *gnaga* and *gnagan*, meaning "to bite or gnaw." One story holds that the term originally derived from the noise rats made chewing away at things inside the walls of houses and ships—where no one could reach them and make them stop!

Sounds about right, doesn't it? When spouses nag each other, it usually feels that way, too—as if, with every nudge and push, every "when are you going to" and "did you remember to" and "don't forget to" and "I wish you'd just," the naggers are carving out another little piece of their partner, going at their mate the way a do-it-yourselfer might take a chisel to a piece of wood: chipping away at flaws, imperfections, and resistance in an effort to shape their partner into the fine, finished carving of a spouse they know their partner can be if they can ... just ... shave ... a little more off—oops! Sorry! Did that hurt?

Nobody enjoys being nagged, and, for all the stereotypes and jokes to the contrary, my experience is that most spouses take no pleasure in feeling put in the position of having to nag, either. Nagging falls into the "bad behavior" category as much as childish behavior and brutal honesty do, and it is equally counterproductive.

I can hear the objections already: "Easy for you to say, but you don't live with my husband! You don't know what it's like being married to a man who [fill in the blank]." I'll get to more constructive ways to deal with whatever you might write in that blank, but first let me review why, no matter what your complaint is, nagging is almost always the wrong way to try to resolve it.

• *It makes your life harder.* Think about it. When you nag your husband about something, anything, it means that on some level, you feel that you are primarily responsible for seeing that whatever it is you're nagging him to do gets done. Instead of letting him carry the weight of that responsibility, you're holding on to it and piling it on top of your already heavy load.

• *It doesn't make you feel good about your partner.* Nagging is a way of saying you don't trust your partner to fulfill his obligations. The more you behave that way, the more you *will* feel that way— and the more he'll feel that you feel that way, too. Instead of chiseling away at his flaws and imperfections, you end up hacking away at the foundation of trust in your marriage.

• *It doesn't make you feel good about yourself.* It makes you feel like what you're acting like: a nag.

• *It often backfires.* Think of how you respond when, say, your mother nudges and needles you about something: "Have you called your aunt Rita yet?" "Did you make an appointment to get a mammogram?" Does it increase your inclination to do the deed? I'd be surprised if it did. If anything, it probably increases your resistance. Probably, you'll get around to making the call or appointment eventually, because you know you have to. Similarly, if you nag your husband to do something—"Have you talked to your boss yet?" or "Did you call about that phone charge?"—and he does it, it's probably because he knew he needed to do it and would have done it anyway. Nagging *might* make get him to do it sooner, if only to get you off his back, but is that the husband you want? One who does things just to get you off his back? Besides, it can also have the opposite effect. Keep nagging, and he may keep postponing, just to let you know he doesn't appreciate being told what to do.

Now, back to that blank you filled in—the specific flaw in your marriage or husband that eats at you the most and causes you to gnaw at your spouse. Here are some alternatives:

• *Do it yourself.* Consider the three-step thinking on this one:

1. If you're bugging him about a task you can handle as capably as he can, if it's an infrequent or one-time thing rather than a regular chore, and if it means more to you than it does to him to see it done at all, much less in a hurry, give him a break, and give yourself a break in the long run: Do it yourself.

2. If it's a task you could do but don't want to do, so you've foisted it off on him, he should be allowed to do it on his timetable.

3. If it's something you could take off his hands but don't want to because why should you give him a break when he never gives you one, or because some part of you likes having something to hold over his head, then admit that this is what's going on and come clean with yourself about why you want him to feel bad. Then read step one again.

• *Negotiate.* If the thing you're nagging your husband about is a routine chore, such as loading the dishwasher every other night, which he's supposed to do and never does, consider that maybe it's his least favorite chore in the world and he'd happily take over some other one if you will just let him out of kitchen duty. If he does the job but doesn't do it to your specifications, it's possible you should back off. Women are often guilty of asking their husbands to take over certain tasks but still wanting to dictate exactly how they should be done. If this is one of your weak points, the next time you're tempted to nag your husband because he dusted around the clock on the mantel instead of lifting it and dusting under it, remind yourself: When he does the dusting, he gets to do it his way.

• *Let it be.* If the task is his to do alone, and it doesn't affect or concern you—you think he should invite the brother he had an argument with to his birthday party but he doesn't want to, or you think he should stop wearing medium-size T-shirts since he now needs to wear an extra-large, but he wears mediums anyway—you get to voice your opinion, gently, once, maybe. But after that: Leave him alone. As I pointed out in Chapter 5, one of the challenges in marriage is respecting differences. Your husband has a right to feel his own feelings and to make his own decisions no matter how certain you are that mother knows best—which is how he'll come to think of you if you continually nag him.

• *Facilitate.* The above examples concern minor issues that have nothing to do with your well-being or your husband's physical well-being. In these cases, nagging him about them says more about you than it does about him. On the other hand, if your husband is putting off doing something truly important—going for a physical, taking his blood-pressure medication daily, getting out there and looking for another job—try to find ways to ease him over his resistance instead of adding to it, which is what nagging mainly does. Offer to make the doctor's appointment for him and go to it with him. Start serving more healthful meals and exercising more yourself. Put the pill on his plate with his dinner. Let him know you're available if he wants help redoing his résumé. Be smart enough to ask *him* to tell *you* how you can help him instead of telling him what he needs to do. He may not have an immediate answer. Let him mull it over, and suggest that you talk about it again in a few days.

• *Remember your vows.* Ask yourself, what if this issue you're pushing your husband to address is something that will never change? What if he has no desire or intention to change in the way you want him to change, and your only choice is to accept him as he is—or not? Don't try to answer that question yet. Remember, you're likely still in the "devaluation" stage of marriage when all flaws and problems may appear magnified. Just tuck the question away in the corner of your heart where you keep your hopes for your marriage. I'll return to it in Chapter 11, after you've moved into the "pride and appreciation" stage and can place these flaws in a better perspective.

4. All the Rusty, Broken, Dangerous Crap in the Junk Drawer: Garbage Fights

Most do-it-yourselfers have a drawer somewhere in which they keep all those broken tools and leftover parts and spare gaskets and flanges and plugs they have no real use for but they don't want to throw away. Call it the "junk drawer." The blade comes off a putty spreader. Could come in handy. Goes in the drawer. A homeowner finds a bolt on the sun porch. Must've come off something. Goes in the drawer. For years these odds and ends accumulate, mostly forgotten, until one day, in the midst of some repair job, a do-it-yourselfer finds herself thinking, *Hmmm. If only I had a blade about so long. Oh! Maybe there's something in the junk drawer!* She riffles through it, dumps out the contents. *No. Darn. But geez! Look at all this junk!*

Most spouses have a drawer somewhere in the back of those prim-itive parts of the brain where they store the marital equivalent of this kind of junk. He forgot to send her flowers at work for her birthday one year. Into the drawer. She wouldn't let his brother borrow her car when he was in town for a few days. Into the drawer. For weeks, months, years, these slights and resentments accumulate. Then one day, the grounds for a disagreement start percolating. A wife tells her husband she's upset because he promised to pick up the dry cleaning on his way home from work, and he didn't, and now the dry cleaner is closed and she doesn't have the suit she wanted to wear to an im-portant meeting the following day. Instead of being sympathetic and apologetic, the husband shrugs it off: "Oh, come on, you have other suits to wear." Now she's more miffed. This is an important meet-ing! She wanted to wear that suit! This is how little he cares about her career? She wants an apology. She wants him to admit he goofed. The more she pushes, the more he stonewalls until, frustrated and even angrier now because nothing she says seems to reach him, she starts casting about for something else to fling at him that will penetrate his thick Neanderthal hide. Ah! The junk drawer! She yanks it open and starts flinging things, nailing him for every bad call, boner mistake, and wrong move he has made since the day they met and before: "You didn't get me an anniversary present last year *and* you got another speeding ticket three months ago *and* you threw out the issue of the *New Yorker* with the Clinton profile in it that I wanted to read *and* you keep leaving your wet towel on the bedroom carpet *and* you brought home the wrong kind of bread yesterday *and* you broke another wineglass this morning *and* you forgot to free the slaves." And so on.

It's pretty obvious that this husband is not going to respond by slapping his forehead and saying, "Gosh, you're right, Mary Todd. Let me go free the slaves, and we'll deal with my complaints about you when I get back." No. He's going to yank his junk drawer open and start flinging things, too: "You keep hanging your pantyhose on the towel rack *and* you scream bloody murder every time I change lanes on the highway *and* you wouldn't let my brother borrow your precious car, which I also partly paid for, when he was in town . . ." And so on.

Sounds funny. But it's not. Spouses who start flinging this kind of junk at each other are in more danger than they think—because once their junk drawers are empty, if the fight isn't over and they're still hopping mad, they reach for bigger, sharper, and heavier things to throw—stuff that can knock holes in walls and crack a foundation:

- "You are *really* turning into your father, do you know that?"

- "No wonder they fired you!"
- "You know what? This is hopeless. I want a divorce."

It doesn't matter if spouses clap their hands over their mouths in horror and fall to their knees begging forgiveness the instant something hurtful escapes their lips. It doesn't matter if the other spouse says, "It's okay, it's okay," either. It's not okay. The damage is done. Here are some ways to avoid getting into "garbage fights":

- Put your hand over your mouth, if that's what it takes, and use every bit of willpower you have to remain calm.

- Stick to the subject at hand. If your partner tries to change the subject, calmly return to it:

You: I'm upset that you forgot to pick up my suit at the cleaners when you said you would.

Him: Yeah, well, I'm upset that you invited your parents to dinner on Sunday without asking me first.

You: Then we should talk about that after we finish this. Let's resolve one thing at a time.

- Resist globalizing, starting sentences with "You always" or "You never." Neither is ever the case.

- Avoid accusing and blaming: "You promised." "You said." "You were supposed to." When has accusing or blaming improved anything in your relationship?

- Resist rhetorical questions: "How could you?" "What were you thinking?" "Why must you always?" They're only accusations in disguise.

• No name-calling or cursing. It's crude, disrespectful to your spouse and marriage, and compromises your maturity and character.

• You can learn to maintain your intensity without ever raising your voice. Believe me, it's a worthy goal.

• Try to resolve things or to jointly agree not to resolve them. Remember, though, that if your husband keeps fending you off and refuses to admit he screwed up, pressing him harder is not going to help. If he's feeling defensive already, he's only going to get more defensive. And, if you keep pushing, your bad behavior trumps his bad behavior—and nobody wins. You're smarter than that, and you can prove it: *retreat*. Say: "Okay. I can see that this isn't helping. I just want you to know I'm disappointed. That's the last thing I'm going to say." If you can back off and drop the subject without turning bitter—that's the challenge, of course—you give him room to relax his guard and reflect, something he can't do when you're hovering over him like a bird over carrion. Will he say the words you want to hear that night? Unlikely. But watch his behavior. Give him time, and he'll probably find a way to show you that he knows what he did, and he doesn't feel good about it.

5. Toxic Chemicals: Poisonous Interactions

Bleach, lye, ammonia, kerosene, spot removers, paint thinner, motor oil, pesticides, lighter fluid. Most homeowners have an array of toxic chemicals in their kitchen, laundry room, bathroom, basement, and garage. As long as these chemicals are carefully sealed, labeled, and stored, they present no significant danger. When something goes wrong, though, when they're not properly sealed, labeled, and stored, when the containers corrode, when these chemicals are misused or mishandled or spill where they shouldn't spill, they can cause serious injury and even death.

Toxic substances accumulate in marriages, too, as a by-product of unnecessarily hurtful couple interactions: the nasty things partners say and do to each other, their sometimes nasty intentions to hurt each other, the nasty ways they interact. In marriage, these toxic substances take the form of resentment, hostility, anger, disgust, and contempt. The less spouses hurt each other, the less of these toxic substances they produce in their relationship. And that's good. Because these toxins are not so easy to store safely. They're volatile, dangerous, and corrosive. Researchers, such as renowned marriage expert John Gottman, who has spent much of his career trying to identify behaviors that help a marriage and behaviors that destroy a marriage, have found that they can predict whether spouses will divorce with a fairly high degree of accuracy simply by observing how the partners interact and argue and watching for evidence of these toxins. Even in small amounts, these substances can pollute the ground a marriage stands on and the air spouses breathe.

In my practice, I sometimes ask couples to rewind a really bad fight they've had all the way back to before it began, and replay it for me so I can help them recognize what each may have done to create these toxic substances and to determine at which point or points they may have let these poisons spill out. The following is a replay of how events unfolded over time for one couple I counseled.

During their first years of married life, Darcy's and Leon's marriage ran so smoothly that they mistakenly if understandably assumed it would always somehow maintain itself. So they began adding on. They had their first child, then (more quickly than planned) their second—followed by their first and second extended bouts of unprecedented exhaustion and unrelenting crankiness, thanks to unanticipated sleep deprivation complicated by the absence of so much as a proper good-night kiss most nights, let alone the physical intimacy they both enjoyed. Over time, their mutual exhaustion and the nonstop demands of parenthood made Darcy and Leon more sensitive and reactive to real *or* imagined slights and offenses. Things that had never been issues between them before became issues: Why didn't Leon clean the bathtub after he took a bath? Did he expect Darcy to do it? Why did Darcy finish Leon's last bottle of ginger ale? Couldn't she have drunk something else? Irritations piled on top of annoyances on top of hurts and frustrations. And then, on a day like any other, something gave: Leon forgot to move the laundry from the washer into the dryer.

It wasn't the first time Leon forgot about the laundry. In the past, when husband and wife were both less stressed, Darcy would switch it to the dryer herself and not even think about it. Or she'd say, "You forgot to switch the laundry again," and then growl to show her annoyance, a playful signal they had worked out. Leon would say, "Oh, I'm sorry, Darce, I swear I think my brain's made of Swiss cheese," and that would be that. Or she would tell him he had to make it up to her by folding all the laundry and putting it away, a task they usually share, and he would agree, and then she would pitch in anyway. And that would be the end of it.

Not this time. This time, Darcy was so tired, so sleep-deprived, so depleted of goodwill and affection, so beyond exhaustion from doing everything she *already* had to do without picking up her husband's slack *again* when he forgot to switch the laundry *again* because, oh sure, Darcy'll do it, just leave it for Darcy, while Leon did *nothing* to help her out . . .

Darcy's toxic feelings toward her husband and marriage had been accumulating, eating at her from the inside, giving off fumes. All it took was a spark of anger and—*ka-boom!*—Darcy exploded: "I am *sooo* sick of this. You have absolutely no consideration for anyone but yourself. All you do is make my life harder."

John Gottman calls this kind of outburst the "harsh setup." Darcy has a point to make, but she drops it like a bomb. There is no opening act, no gentle preface—the attack seems to come out of nowhere and nothing.

Leon, meanwhile, had no idea it was coming. One minute he was minding his own business, doing his best, trying to hold up his end, and the next minute—*ka-boom!*—he's splattered with toxins. Toxins on his skin, in his eyes, in his mouth, in his hair. And for what? Because he forgot to switch the laundry to the dryer? For that, he got this? On another night, Leon might have given Darcy a pass on her outburst. He might have grabbed a towel, wiped himself off, and walked away, or even tried to soothe her: "Gosh, Darcy, I'm sorry, I really am. I promised to do it, and I screwed up again."

But not this time. Uh-uh. On this night, Leon was just as exhausted as Darcy was, and yes, he forgot about the laundry—again—but what about everything he *remembered* to do, huh? What about that? Who did the dishes and took out the trash and shopped for groceries on the way home and got dinner started while Darcy picked up the kids at the sitter? Leon had just as much on his plate as she did, and he was tired of her always getting upset about the one thing he forgot to do and never giving him credit for everything he *did* do. Give her a pass? Apologize? Forget it. Instead he came back with: "Oh, no! I forgot to switch the laundry! Why don't you just buy a gun and shoot me? How the hell am I supposed to remember to switch the laundry when I'm so busy doing the ten other things on Darcy's daily list of orders for Leon: 'Leon do this. Leon do that. Leon, jump up and don't come down until I tell you to.' "

Now Leon was spewing toxic chemicals, too. Gottman calls this kind of poisonous rejoinder the "sarcastic comeback."

On another day, Darcy would have sniffed the air, looked at the floor, and run for a mop and bucket. She would have realized that she and Leon were both exhausted and tried to soften things: "Leon, let's take a break, okay? We're both tired and whatever I say now is going to come out wrong. How about we both cool off and talk again in an hour?"

Softening, as it's commonly called, is a way for spouses to signal to each other that there's a problem they know they need to address, but now doesn't seem to be a good time to do it. They're not blowing each other off. They're simply saying that, out of respect for their marriage, it's probably a good idea to take a break, calm down, and come back to the problem later.

But Darcy was in no mood to be so wise and magnanimous that day. *Darcy's list of orders for Leon*, she thought. *How dare he? If he would just take a look around once in a while and see what needs doing I wouldn't have to— Aww, screw it. I don't need this*. Darcy narrowed her eyes at Leon, pressed her lips together—uh-oh, he knew what that look meant—and turned and walked out of the living room. *That's it*, she thought. *Why waste my breath. There's no point talking to him—ever*. Darcy reached for her inner tank of Freon—another dangerous chemical—opened the gasket, and—*phffffffft*—froze her husband out. When he followed her into the kitchen, she turned around and walked upstairs. She would not speak to him or look at him, and she waved him off angrily when he followed her wanting to finish this discussion, damn it. She was as sweet and loving as ever with the kids, but forget him. When she needed to address him, she did so by talking to them: "Jeffrey, honey, could you tell the lord of the manor that dinner's ready, please."

"Who, Mommy?"

"Daddy. Tell Daddy it's time to eat."

Darcy was filling the air in their home, up where she and Leon breathed it, with the toxic substance called "the silent treatment." And Leon was starting to choke. However, Leon would probably admit that this was preferable to her other favorite tactic—following Leon around the house, chattering nonstop about the many ways he'd ruined her life, about how she could have married Freddy or any number of others.

On a good day, Leon would recognize that the only sensible thing to do was to make a conciliatory gesture: "Come on, Darce, we're better than this. I'm sorry I got nasty. Let's not do this to each other, okay?" But not that day. That day, he was so worked up, so furious, so red-in-the-face with anger at being frozen out that instead of coming to the table for dinner when his son came to get him, he told his son, "That's okay, pal. You go eat. Daddy has to go out." And he grabbed his jacket and car keys and left, slamming the door.

Leon had reached the stage where he was too physiologically worked up to be able to think clearly. He actually did the right thing by going off to give himself time to calm down. But he did it the wrong way.

Leon drove to the mall and spent an hour wandering the aisles of a sporting goods store. He picked up a new Wiffle ball and bat for the kids. On the way home, he stopped in the supermarket for the carton of orange juice he forgot to get when he shopped earlier. He spent another fifteen minutes browsing the magazine rack, picked up a *Sports Illustrated* for himself and a *Vogue* for Darcy—he knew how much she liked to look at the clothes—and finally headed home. He was calmed down now, and he was feeling bad about their fight. By the time he got home, Darcy had the kids in bed, and she was in the kitchen cleaning up. Leon put the orange juice and magazines on the table and went to hug her, but she stiff-armed him and gave him a withering look. "Go away," she told him huskily. "Just leave me alone. This is how you treat me? You just walk out and leave me here with the kids? Don't even talk to me. You're a bigger loser than I even thought."

Darcy had now thrown acid at Leon and all over the marriage. She was telling him he disgusted her, that he was inferior and worthless. She was treating him with outright contempt, the most toxic substance of all.

Safety First!

Darcy's and Leon's marriage was damaged by this ugly fight, but it was not destroyed. Humbled and frightened that they had let things get so disastrously out of control, they both worked hard during our counseling session to identify the various points during the fight when each of them had had a choice—escalate or deescalate, ratchet up or ratchet down, put pride first or put the marriage first—and had each made the wrong choice. More than once.

In Part 3 I'll go into more detail about how spouses can avoid letting arguments get to this dangerous stage, and what they can do if they find themselves caught up in a fight that has gone this far. For now, remember this:

Anger itself is not toxic. Neither is fighting. We all know couples who seem to fight all the time yet still swear that they are happy. They may not be pleasant to have over for Thanksgiving dinner, but that's not the point. The point is that anger is normal and fighting is normal. Neither in itself is damaging to a marriage. It's *how* couples fight and *how* they express their anger that determines whether they will do harm to their marriage. That's where each partner's ability to maintain control rather than lose control, to think before acting rather than act without thinking, becomes crucial.

All spouses know how to escalate a fight. That's not difficult. The hard part is resisting the urge to do it. Most spouses can come up with a good, cutting remark when their blood is boiling, too. That's easy. The hard part is swallowing the vicious words instead of spitting them out.

Here's the simple truth about marital fights: The most important fight you will ever have is the fight you have with yourself *before* you speak, *before* you attack, *before* you escalate or retaliate, *before* you let those razor-sharp words fly out of your mouth. You and your spouse will both be called on to wage this battle with yourselves over and over. Fight hard. Fight to win. You're fighting for your marriage.

Now that you've assembled the tools and skills you need to make lasting marriage repairs—and tossed out the ones that do more harm than good—you're ready to get to work. Why not start in the bedroom? In the next chapter, I'll talk about how to improve your marriage's heating system: your sex life.

PART 3

Major Repairs

CHAPTER 7

Sex: If It Isn't Hot, You Should Be Bothered

How to Fire Up the Furnace and Keep the Heat Flowing

Imagine, for a moment, that a woman wakes at the crack of dawn one winter morning because her toes are freezing. She reaches down to pull back the blanket that her husband always manages to pull off her side of the bed and onto his, and realizes it isn't just her toes—her whole body is cold. She knows what's happened: That damned old furnace isn't working again. She jumps up to throw extra blankets over the sleeping kids and to make sure the parakeet is still alive. Then, she comes back to the bedroom. "Honey, wake up. There's no heat," she says, shaking her husband. He slowly wakes, realizes that he can actually see his breath in puffy white clouds, and jumps up, echoing her concern: "Damn! I hope it's not the furnace," he says. "Can you check the thermostat?" And they climb into their robes and slippers, one heading for the thermostat, the other heading for the basement with a flashlight.

To their dismay, the thermostat shows a chilly 48 degrees, and the furnace won't reboot with a flipping of the red switch; this time it's really shot. Shivering, the husband and wife convene in the kitchen and immediately dial the furnace repair number—and keep dialing it every half hour until someone shows up. What other choice do they have? What husband and wife would sigh in resignation, pile on a few layers of sweaters, pants, and socks, and (despite their blue lips) go back to sleep? Who would shrug and say, "Oh, it's only three months until spring—we can make it"?

Nobody!

A mutually satisfying sex life is the crucial, central heating system in a relationship. And if it were up to me, spouses would be just as quick to act when the heat goes off in their marriage—that is, when their sex life goes on the blink. Sadly, though, that's often not how they respond. For numerous understandable but unfortunate reasons, this is a marriage repair that many couples find especially difficult to acknowledge and address.

In the romantic stage of love and marriage, heat kicks on by itself, multiple times a day, keeping things hot and glistening in the bedroom. Eventually, though, outside obligations—not to mention hunger for other things, like food—start knocking on the bedroom door, and force spouses to leave the bedroom (but not thoughts of it) and start putting their energy into other matters, such as going to work, cooking and cleaning, handling finances, dealing with relatives, and raising kids. Over time, the more involved a couple gets in more public aspects of their life, the more likely it is that there will to be a heat transfer from the bedroom to, say, the boardroom or other arenas. What happens then? Often, the slightly more neglected partner turns the heat down slightly in the bedroom. Then, the other partner slips it down one more degree, to get even.

Usually, they don't even notice at first. But then they start to—and then they start lowering the heat even more, if that's possible.

This is childish behavior, of course. Instead of reaching for more constructive tools, such as staying calm and becoming curious rather than defensive, it's a way of responding to a marital problem by reaching for the destructive tin-toy tools of "acting out." Counterproductive as this can be, it happens. Back and forth a husband and wife can go until, one morning, they wake up with a few icicles on their ceiling. And instead of turning to each other and saying, "Hold me, I'm cold," they do nothing. Or they go back to sleep.

So, they begin to read Victorian novels or become existential about it or go to the gym more or figure this happens to everyone as they get older. They'll make the best of it, they tell themselves. After all, it's not freezing cold. Just . . . chilly. They still love each other. They're still affectionate. Don't they always hold hands? Things could be worse.

Yes, they could—they nearly always could. But in most cases, things could also be better, a lot better, if spouses would pay as much attention to their sex life as to a broken furnace, and keep talking and attempting to solve the problem until it gets fixed. Why do spouses find this so difficult to do when it comes to sex? Because sex, of course, is a touchy subject. No human activity is riddled with more confusion, anxiety, timidity, or angst.

When I was a younger therapist, I thought that if partners both seemed happy in a sexless marriage, that was all that mattered. As I gained experience, however, I came to see that many spouses settle into this arrangement not because it's what they really want (even when they say they do), but because they've made an unspoken pact not to deal with the issue.

I once led a workshop in Chicago for couples who were contending with erectile dysfunction (ED) in their marriages. This workshop opened my eyes both to how far couples can go to not break this silence and what the costs can be. ED is a problem that afflicts men and couples of all ages and lifestyles, by the way. Some of the couples at this workshop were older, but many were younger. Many, even in their thirties, had gone years with no sexual contact.

At the beginning of the workshop, I separated the men from the women, organized them into small discussion groups, and asked each group to report back on the most important things said within the group. The single most important revelation: Several men and women admitted that their marriages almost broke up before the men sought help for their problem—not because of the lack of sex, but because the husband and wife couldn't talk about it. This inability to name and discuss the problem caused both marital partners to begin thinking and acting in defensive and anxious ways that only strained their marriage even more. Husbands retreated into feigned lack of interest or defensive antagonism toward their wives. Women, being women, blamed themselves. One woman decided it was the ten pounds she had gained. Another became convinced her husband was having an affair. Another decided her marriage was simply over: Sex was how her husband showed love, and no sex, to her, meant no love. She had begun gathering names of good divorce lawyers when her husband finally said: "I've been putting this off, but can we talk?" Amazingly, for almost all of these couples, as soon as the husband or the wife finally summoned the courage to break through this wall of silence, name the problem, and transform it into something they could face as a couple, they were able to comfort each other, seek help, and start down the path of repair (and sex). The very fact that these couples attended the workshop was evidence of that.

The bottom line: It's not lack of sex that destroys a marriage. It's how much the connection between spouses suffers as a result of not talking about it. When the heat goes off and partners can't look at each other and say, "I'm cold. Are you cold?" the problem gets worse. Let the temperature in a house or marriage plummet low enough, and eventually the pipes freeze—and then burst.

Some Like It Hot—And Some Don't

There is no single correct sexual thermostat setting for all couples, of course. Some like it very hot. Some like it cooler. Some like it somewhere in between.

• Marian and Bobby were never that into sex. When they began dating seriously, they had sex more than either had ever had before, out of a desire to please each other. (Remember the O. Henry story "Gift of the Magi"?) When it finally came out that neither of them really cared that much about it, they had a good laugh and realized what a perfect match they were.

• Bart and Sylvia, on the other hand, have been married for twenty-seven years and still have sex every weekday and more than once a day on weekends. They did the math once for the fun of it and calculated that they've had sex more than 12,000 times. "And we're just getting warmed up," Bart said, laughing and grabbing his beaming wife's hand.

• Wendy and Rick are both okay with their once-a-month Saturday-night date. They like the anticipation. They like knowing that when that special Saturday evening rolls around, it's completely theirs. They like the rituals they've developed: lighting candles, taking a bath together, sipping champagne, stripping each other, sharing fantasies, massaging each other with their favorite oil. They enjoy taking their sweet time with sex and lingering in the afterglow.

• With two jobs and three young kids, Perry and Jake know they can't afford to wait until they have time for sex, so two or three nights a week, they *make* time—even it's a quickie at six AM or eleven thirty PM, even if one or both fall asleep immediately after . . . or during.

• Sue and Luis play a game that turns them both on, silly as they both know it is: When she feels the itch, she calls, "Oh, Luuuuiii-issss" to give him warning and then comes after him and literally chases him around the house. Wherever she corners him—or he lets himself be cornered—that's where they have sex.

• Bonnie and Alf like to act out fantasy scenarios complete with costumes and props: nurse-doctor, master-slave, international spies. They like sex toys, especially ones that glow in the dark, and like to watch erotic movies, too. There isn't much they won't try, as long as it's just the two of them, which it always is. That's their deal.

As for you, whatever goes on behind your bedroom door (I know one couple who bought an antique carousel horse for the wife's Lady Godiva fantasy) is fine, as long as you and your spouse are open and talkative enough about it and happy enough with it—not only pretending to be. If, on the other hand, the two of you started out slip-sliding together but now you barely touch, don't settle for a sex life made up mostly of memories. The truth is:

- The loss of your sexual connection is likely a loss for you both.
- Sexual activity promotes physical and emotional health.
- Sex can be an oasis for partners in a sea of stress and responsibilities.
- Sex is powerful glue between partners and can help a marriage thrive.
- Unsatisfied sexual desire can destabilize a marriage, however much spouses may not want to face that fact.

"Me? Cold? No, I'm Not Cold. Are You Cold?"
Four Reasons the Sexual Heat Fails

When the heat goes off in a house, homeowners or repair people have to locate the source of the problem before they can fix it. Here are four common reasons that spouses turn the sexual heat in their marriage down so low that it can sputter out.

1. Why heat rooms you don't use? It's not uncommon for families living in large or drafty houses to save on fuel costs in winter by turning the thermostat way down in the rooms they don't have to use and keeping it set higher in the ones they do use. Something similar happens between spouses when they start a family. Babies and small children demand an incredible amount of care and attention—from Mom especially, who still tends to be the primary caretaker. She's not going to be visiting her marital bed for much of anything, except to collapse into it for what is never long enough. She needs the heat to be pumping into the baby's room more than the bedroom. So what if the bedroom isn't as hot as it used to be? Who has the time or energy to notice!

Dad does, of course. Not immediately, perhaps. For the first three to six months or so of new parenthood, husbands and wives are usually too overwhelmed by the responsibilities of caring for the baby to think much about sex. But for husbands, especially, that sexual time-out period is finite. Early on, he gets the picture that his wife's love for the baby is different and all-consuming. He feels it, too—but his penis has a life of its own and is completely comfortable with asking for attention, infant or no infant. Often, right around this same six-month mark—sometimes sooner, sometimes later—Mom also starts missing the pleasures of sexual intimacy, on those rare occasions when she wakes up refreshed enough to realize, "Gosh, I don't think we've had sex since the Clinton administration." The problem is, when she does wake up that refreshed, it's usually because Dad has taken the kids off her hands for a few hours to give her a break. This common marital pattern of trading off childcare creates all sorts of opportunities for miscommunication, because it puts Mom and Dad on sexual swing shifts: Either he's in the bedroom alone, awake and ready for some adult fun, or she is. Either she's too preoccupied with the kids to join him there, or vice versa. The end result: They're never in the bedroom together long enough when they're awake enough to turn to each other and say, "I'm cold. Are you cold?" or "Brrrr, let's warm each other up." And, depending on the mom and the dad, the level of partnership in the marriage in terms of tasks and responsibilities, and the dependency issues of the dependents, this can go on for months and, sometimes, years. Yes, years—as the temperature in the bedroom slowly drops until the room feels like a little igloo at the North Pole.

Karen and Arthur, a couple who came to see me earlier this year, struggle with this constantly. Karen, a stay-at-home mom, is exhausted all week from caring for their six-year-old son and three-year-old daughter. Arthur can get resentful that this leaves her with so little energy for him, but what's he going to do? Arthur has a long commute and barely sees his kids during the week, so on weekends he enjoys taking over the bulk of the childcare and giving Karen a chance to sleep late and take the first shower she's had in days in which she actually gets to stay in long enough to wash all the shampoo out of her hair.

One especially quiet Sunday afternoon, as Arthur went off to settle the kids for a nap, Karen started to feel those low stirrings. "Know what?" she told her husband. "After you put the kids down, how about we take a nap, too?" Karen was signaling to him that she wanted to have sex, but because Arthur was wrapped up in the kids, he missed the signal. Ten minutes later, he came into their bedroom with both kids in his arms. "What the heck," he said, smiling. "I get so little time with them. How about we all take a nap together?" Karen didn't say anything, but she had wanted this to be their time. Who knew when they'd have a chance like it again? The events of that afternoon got stored in Karen's marital junk drawer, to be thrown back at Arthur, along with all the other spare hurts and loose insults stored there, the next time they got into the kind of "garbage fight" I described in Chapter 6.

Couples like Karen and Arthur could fill a book with these mis-read signals. They are the reason that planning a specific time for sex makes so much sense, as unromantic as it sounds. With kids and work schedules, timing cannot be left to chance, because there is never a "perfect moment" (until the kids go off to college, at least).

2. Steamy bedroom and comfy home: It's not easy to have both.
Over the course of twenty years of professional practice, I've developed several theories about why the temperature drops in so many

marital bedrooms. When I began writing this book, I decided to test one of these theories by doing a little anecdotal experiment. I e-mailed about ten married couples I know and asked them to answer two questions. First, I asked them to describe their idea of an ideal home— to tell me what kind of family life they'd like to return to at the end of a long day. Except for the woman who said she wanted to come home to George Clooney, most of the men and women said pretty much the same thing. Ideally, they wanted their home life to be cozy, peaceful, quiet, safe, comfortable, and relaxing. Then I asked them to describe great sex—what they'd like their sex life to be like. Except for the woman who repeated "George Clooney," most of the men and women again said pretty much the same thing—except, this time, the words they came up were very different. A great sex life, they said, should be hot, spontaneous, passionate, wild, kinky, and uninhibited.

Let's compare these lists:

Ideal Home Life	**Ideal Sex Life**
Cozy	Kinky
Peaceful	Passionate
Quiet	Wild
Safe	Spontaneous
Comfortable	Uninhibited
Relaxing	Hot

It doesn't take a Rhodes scholar to see that these lists are incompatible. Spouses want their marriage and family life to be safe and secure, but they want their sex life to be wild and crazy. They want their family life to be a rose-covered cottage, but they want their sex life to be a bordello. They want the family rooms to be cozy, but they want the bedroom to be steamy.

There's the rub, because, to achieve this, couples must figure out how to heat-seal the bedroom to keep steamy in and cozy out. And when does a couple get to sit down and figure this out? Even if they mean to? Without even realizing it, they open the bedroom door, and steamy escapes and cozy seeps in. Adventurous slips out and predictable slips in. X-rated slips out and G-rated slips in. Sex becomes comforting ... but not that exciting. Sweet ... but not really sexy.

While it's not reasonable for couples to keep the bedroom steamy all the time, it is quite reasonable to want to find ways to boost the temperature in a hurry once they've closed the bedroom door. The first step in that sweaty direction is one simple but powerful strategy: *Preserve your bedroom for sleeping and sex only*.

Everything that you allow in your bedroom, from people to pillows to pictures, should be judged according to whether it enhances or detracts from the pleasures of sleeping and sex—particularly sex. Your bedroom should not also function as the children's play room (no toy boxes near the night table, unless those "toys" are very adult), or a home office if you can help it, or a TV-watching room, no matter how tempting that is, or the museum of family history. Display the framed family photos elsewhere—not on your bedroom bureau or walls. Nothing can kill that rising steam heat faster than having your eyes land on a photo of your mom and dad—or worse, *his mom and dad*—the exact moment he pulls your panties off.

3. Problems with heat distribution: blockages in the pipes, fans, and vents. Sometimes when homeowners wake up chilly in their bedrooms they'll check the vents and find they are cold. Then they'll check the thermostat but find it's set right. Hmmm. Must be the furnace. They'll go down to the basement and touch the furnace. Nope, it's not the furnace—the furnace is plenty hot. It must be some problem with heat distribution, they surmise, some blockage or backup in the pipes or vents.

When the sexual temperature drops in a marriage, spouses often feel the "vents" (one or both partner's seeming lack of interest or arousal), they check the "thermostat" (their failed attempts to warm up their spouse), and they conclude that the problem must be the furnace: their basic physical desire for each other, the essential source of their sexual heat. However, if they could touch each other's furnaces, they would know the truth instantly. Nope! The heat hasn't died. The desire is still there. The problem isn't the heat. It's the distribution: some undiagnosed physical or physiological blockage that can look like lack of desire in men and women both.

You'd think that with all the television commercials and magazine ads discussing ED so openly these days, men would find it easier to seek help for erectile problems and other sexual concerns. But many still don't. Just a few months ago, while walking my two cairn terriers, Sparky and Scarlett, I stopped at my local flower shop to chat with the proprietor, a forty-eight-year-old man named Tony who always has biscuits for the dogs. I've been stopping there several times a month for ten years. During that time, Tony, who knows I'm a therapist, has talked a lot about his marriage to his beautiful wife. (I've seen her picture. She really is beautiful.) On this day, however, after feeding and petting the dogs, Tony glanced around to make sure no one was in earshot and said he was glad to see me because there was something he wanted to ask me about. He proceeded to tell me that, for the last few months and for the first time in thirteen years of marriage, he'd lost all interest in sex. He and his wife used to have sex every day, he said. The very sight of her was enough to excite him. But now—nothing. "But maybe that's what happens after you've been married for a while," he said. "Or maybe that's what happens when you get older. I am almost fifty now." What did I think?

I asked him what his wife thought. He frowned. "We haven't talked about it," he said. "But I know she's not happy." I asked if he had talked to his doctor. He frowned again. "No. How could that help?"

I told him I absolutely thought he should. In my practice and when I lecture, I always encourage men who are having erectile difficulties to get a full physical exam to make sure the problem isn't medically based. Diabetes, high blood pressure, depression, cardiac problems, prostate problems, drinking, and drug use are just a few conditions that can cause erectile problems. ED can also be a side effect of certain treatments and therapies, such as chemotherapy and taking certain medications, including some antidepressants. A man can fail to get an erection because he's depressed and then, by taking antidepressants, he can actually lose what was left of his interest in sex. But, with good medical treatment, the best balance of medication can be found—one that eases his depression but still lets his libido lambada. Of course, this requires looking for a doctor who is willing to work closely with him on this issue and who takes his concerns seriously. Simply having the degree of MD does not mean a doctor is comfortable talking about sex. A man who needs help in this area needs to find one who is.

Women also experience reduced sexual desire and responsiveness due to conditions such as depression or reduced hormonal function, or as a side effect of taking certain medicines—and these problems often go undiagnosed and untreated when doctors aren't told about them. The list of medications that can inhibit sexual interest and function is long, but doctors often don't think to mention these possible side effects unless patients ask. If the problem is a medicine a woman is taking, her physician might be able to switch her to another, or the solution may be something as simple as taking the same medicine at a different time of day. As a rule, women don't find it any easier to discuss sexual problems with doctors than men do, but, trust me, a doctor who is the right one for you has had these conversations with patients many times.

Talking with a physician can also help men and women figure out if they're panicking about something over which there's really no reason to panic, and help them to stay calm, keep a cool head, and not exaggerate or overreact. What my friend Tony, for example, described as a sudden and complete loss of interest in sex might not be anything like that at all. It could simply be, as I told him, that what used to turn him on instantly—the mere sight of his beautiful wife—doesn't have the same effect anymore, and he and his wife need to experiment with other forms of stimulation. I'll return to this point later, too.

4. Turning off the heat on purpose: when spouses freeze each other out. Spouses who are unable to express hurt and anger directly sometimes use sex to drive their partner away—either knowingly or unknowingly, as if they were walking over to the thermostat and shutting it off in their sleep.

In Chapter 3, I described a former female client who never walked out her front door on a workday looking anything less than perfect but who abandoned even the most basic standards of hygiene on weekends because she was so angry at her husband that she wanted to keep him at arm's length. In that case, the woman came to me complaining of depression, and only later connected her depression (her anger turned inward) and troubling behaviors to her anger at her mate.

In another case, a man named William came to see me because he was worried about the way his wife, Corrine, was letting herself go. He wasn't talking about the fifteen pounds she was still carrying since the birth of their third child, he said. He actually liked her a little plumper. But for the last six months or so Corrine had been living in one of two sets of grungy old T-shirts and sweatpants, both outfits baggy, droopy, and covered with stains. She also walked around barefoot throughout the day and her feet were always filthy. William didn't know what to say and wasn't sure he had a right to say anything, because Corrine was the one who was home with the kids all day while he was at work. One night he decided to surprise her with a candlelit bubble bath. He filled the tub, lit the candles, and walked her into the bathroom with her eyes closed. "You should have seen her face," he said, smiling. He told her to take her time and soak as long as she wanted—he'd take care of the kids. "She threw her arms around my neck and gave me a big kiss, she was so grateful," he said. William had hoped that when Corrine emerged from the bath, relaxed, refreshed, and sparkling clean, she would want to maintain the feeling by putting on fresh, sparkling clean clothes, too. He had also hoped that the bubble bath would stir her memories of the bubble baths they used to take together before the kids came along—maybe reawaken her desire for the fabulous sex that always followed. But neither happened. "When she got out of the tub, she put the same T-shirt and sweatpants back on," William told me. "Not even the clean set—the dirty one. I swear I could smell baby spit-up on the shirt." William didn't know what else to do, so he had come to see me.

On his next visit he brought Corrine with him, and the two of them entered counseling. It soon emerged that before they married, William and Corrine had agreed that they wanted a traditional family life: He'd work and she'd stay home. In reality, though, being home with three children every day was making Corrine extremely unhappy. She'd mentioned going back to work once, early on, but when William did the math, he said it would be better for her to stay home because she wouldn't earn enough money to break even if they got a full-time nanny. If William had responded to his wife's overture with curiosity ("Tell me more") instead of defensiveness ("We can't afford it"), as discussed in Chapter 5, Corrine would have had a chance to explain how desperately she needed a break from being home all the time. But he didn't, and she didn't press it. Instead, she went along with him, her resentment building, while inwardly she fumed because she felt so intellectually understimulated. And because William was also somewhat deficient in paying real attention to his wife and developing empathy for her, he remained oblivious to her growing unhappiness. Wrapped up in his good job, he thought Corrine had become tired and cranky—for six years straight. (This does happen.) It came down to the fact that she and William needed to revise their marriage plan, but Corrine didn't know how to tell William this. In addition, Corrine had hated it when her own mom worked when she was growing up, so she had tried to suck it up and make the best of things. When, finally, she and William began negotiating the issue, she decided to get a part-time job. William assured her he wanted his lover back. Screw the math!

It isn't always the case that spouses who let their appearances go are acting out some deep unhappiness, though. Sometimes, especially in the case of stay-at-home moms, they're simply not thinking about their appearances. They don't turn off the thermostat in the bedroom on purpose, in other words. They knock it off accidentally as they're doing a million things, and then drop into bed at night in such a dead heap that they don't even realize the heat's off unless their mate says something.

This is a problem, but it's not a big problem—and, as I mentioned in Chapter 5, one of the traits of a good do-it-yourselfer is to examine a problem and try the simplest solution first. In this case, the simplest solution is for a husband (or wife) to find a way to *sensitively* express their *positive* desire for each other to pay more attention to appearance: "Your hair always looks so beautiful after you've washed it. Want to take a shower together, and I can wash it for you?" "You have the cutest butt. I love when you wear clothes that show it off." "Let's take a walk after dinner. I could use the exercise." If this doesn't work after multiple tries, one partner may need to address the problem more directly, but it should be done very, very gently: "I want to say something. I love you and I don't want to hurt your feelings, yet I've wondered lately if . . ." Sometimes, that's all it takes to shake partners out of these bad habits. Because sometimes that's all they are: bad habits that spouses need to be called on.

Finally, some spouses who turn off the bedroom thermostat don't fall into either of these two groups: They're not suffering from deep, unidentified unhappiness; and they haven't slipped into bad habits unaware. They've turned off the heat on purpose and they know exactly why. They're doing it either to avoid sex specifically because they don't like it, or don't like it with their partner, or they don't want to get pregnant and abstinence is the only birth control they use; or because they want to punish their partner for a sin or transgression they could name but won't—another of those childish, tin-toy tool behaviors I talked about in Chapter 6. If you've turned off the sexual

When Sabina and Marco came into counseling, both had grown increasingly dissatisfied with their sex life. Sabina complained that since the birth of their daughter, then twenty months old, Marco's job as a bookseller for a major publishing conglomerate kept him on the road more than ever. Before their daughter was born, he'd be gone two, maybe three nights a week. Now he was usually gone Monday through Friday, meaning that Sabina was home alone with the baby all week. When Marco did show up on Friday night, she complained, he expected her to greet him at the door in what he called "an outfit" and pounce on him, just because he was home. Marco reminded Sabina—and he couldn't believe he *had* to remind her—that he had warned her he'd be on the road more if he took his most recent promotion, and that they had agreed he should accept it because, with a child to support and Sabina working only a couple of afternoons a week in a bookstore, they needed the money. He didn't like being away all week any more than she did, he said, but did she have a better solution? And after four nights in a row of sleeping alone in motels, was it so unreasonable to want to come home and have sex with his wife?

Sabina snapped. "You think I don't miss having sex, too? It's just, every Friday night, like clockwork: Marco's home! Time for sex!" She made a face. "I'm sorry, but that does *not* turn me on. I want things to be spontaneous, like they used to be."

Sabina's feelings were understandable, but impractical. There was no way for her to get her wish. They had about forty-eight hours a week to renew their sexual bond. Subtract the hours the baby was awake and needy, and it came to a lot less. If she wasn't willing to plan, she and Marco might not have sex again for a long time.

Even so, Sabina said she still couldn't settle for clockwork sex every Friday night, but she and Marco did begin to cooperate, working together until they devised a plan that pleased them both (enough). They agreed that they would definitely have sex at least twice each weekend. Marco would be in charge of two weekends a month and Sabina would be in charge of the others. In a five-weekend month, they'd throw dice for the odd weekend. They also agreed that on Marco's weekends, he'd "stroke the mind before he stroked the behind." This meant he'd call Sabina on his cell from the car and describe what he was looking forward to doing to her, and having her do to him (something they'd both established in the past as a definite turn-on for Sabina). This preamble to Friday-night sex turned out to be incredibly effective, Sabina said later. "It gave me time to anticipate and fantasize," she said, "and that changed everything."

Spontaneous sex is delicious, but once spouses emerge from the romantic stage of marriage, the distractions and demands of daily life don't leave much time for it. And the hard, exhausting, incredibly rewarding work of raising a family asks so much of couples that they simply can't afford to leave sex entirely to chance. But there are all kinds of ways to work it in. Rick and Laurie always put their toddler down for a Saturday nap. Billie and Sam have worked out a Friday-night babysitting swap with the couple next door. Jane and Henry drop the kids at her parents' house for an overnight stay once a month.

You and your husband do not have endless stretches of time for sex. You have small windows of opportunity. Know what they are, and plan ahead to use them well.

2. Is it time to fiddle with some dials and knobs? In your house, you will fiddle around with the thermostat when it gets chilly, searching to find the setting that feels just right. In a long-term relationship, couples should expect to make regular sexual adjustments, too, because arousal changes over a lifetime. There are points when it's all about what you see—such as your partner's fabulous body. There are times when it's all about what you hear—either those delicious sweet nothings or his offer to do the dishes gets you hot. There are times when he smells great and that is the turn-on, or when he doesn't smell great and *that* is the turn on. Then there's you—and those times your furnace may take longer to fire up, so to speak, and deliver heat to all those outlying areas that need to get good and hot before the party can begin. Your knobs may need more direct handling than they did before. Expect to play around until the right nooks and crannies get massaged into full-blown passion. What you may be experiencing are sexual changes—not the sexual deadening you thought was occurring. Spouses who take these changes in stride and adopt a curious and playful approach to altering their sexual practices position themselves well (literally and figuratively) for enjoying renewed lust and satisfaction.

However, the first step—the step where each partner takes responsibility for his or her own sexual pleasure—isn't easy. A key component of this step is learning to say what you *really* want, where you want it, how you want it, and how long you want it for. For many men and women, this feels scary because it is so intimate, and may even feel like their secret to keep. Without sharing this information, though, your sex life can't grow to the stage of mutuality, where the two of you bring your true desires to each other with the intention to please your partner and yourself. For example, if these days twice as much foreplay is needed for you to warm up because you're so preoccupied with worries about the kids, say so! Don't you think he'd rather know this, than be left to conclude from all physical signs that you're not as interested in him as you once were? Maybe you need more stimulation than he can provide—like a vibrator or watching an erotic video. Would you enjoy sex more if you and your spouse could agree that it isn't always crucial that you both have an orgasm? Do you want to use a few more four-letter words besides "love"? Would you rather he didn't? Want to surprise him from time to time by putting on a Mary J. Blige wig or other accessory? Never mind what you and your partner *used to* like. What works *now*?

Answering the following questions can help you and your husband clarify what it takes to put you in the mood and keep you there. They work best if you encourage him to answer them as well, comparing and discussing your answers as you go. (If you're too shy to discuss them out loud, perhaps you can write down your answers and exchange the papers instead—diagrams included.)

- What are the three best sexual experiences you have had together during the past year?
- What made them the best? Be specific.
- How do you need to be touched or stimulated to become aroused, and how much time do you think it might take? Be specific.
- Provide details of what turns you on *now*.
- If you could design the perfect erotic sexual encounter with your partner, what would it be? Elaborate.
- How do you let your partner know when you want to have an orgasm and what you need him to do for you to have one?
- How do you let your partner know when you're content without having an orgasm?
- What haven't you told your partner about your sexual desires, fantasies, and preferences that he should know?

3. Do you know how to relight your own pilot light? In the beginning of a relationship, the pilot light of sexual desire is always on, and the flame never flickers. He blinks. She's hot. She sweats. He's hot. He laughs. She's hot. With time, however, even the best pilot light will usually sputter, and one partner's desire will not be enough to ignite the other's. A couple may go a while (weeks, months, years, even) with no temperature spike. What's a long-married couple supposed to do when they hit one of these dry spells? *Have sex anyway!* If the heat isn't on tap, they should start without it. This does require an initial act of will, but couples who do it are liable to discover the paradox of married sex: Partners who don't initially feel all hot and bothered about having sex often find that *having sex is what gets them all hot and bothered.* They don't just *have* it because they *want* it. They *want* it because they *have* it.

When I suggested this strategy to Olivia and Gary, who had hit their first *loooong* dry spell after seven years of marriage, Gary was willing to give it a try—but Olivia resisted, feeling she should not have to force it. So they went without sex for another week, and then another, and another. Olivia was convinced, she admitted later, that if they went long enough without sex certainly their hunger would return, but that didn't happen. Remember that old blues tune "Use It or Lose It"? Sexual appetites can go dormant. Waiting two weeks might help. Waiting two months does not.

Fortunately, after four weeks, Olivia reconsidered and decided to give Gary what she privately thought of as "mercy sex." It wouldn't kill her, she thought, to give him oral sex without asking anything in return.

The following Saturday night, both she and Gary were in for a big surprise because, as Olivia focused on arousing Gary with no pressure to join him, and as Gary became more aroused, her red switch got flipped on, too. "Seeing him get so excited, having that effect on him, was a total turn-on," she said. That night ended up being very hot for both of them, she added—and it taught them something they were very glad to learn. Until then, Gary had almost always initiated sex; neither of them had realized that doing a 180 would be such an aphrodisiac for the two of them.

4. Do you need to become better friends with your furnace?
Some homeowners may decide that furnaces are huge, gross, ugly, smelly things that they simply do not want anything to do with. If they could move someplace where they'd never need to own one, they'd be glad. Sometimes, women (far more than men) have that kind of attitude toward their own bodies. They're so self-critical that they can't help letting these feelings spill over into sex. Some common ways women letting these feelings show are:

- They don't like to undress in front of their husband.
- They don't want their husband to see them naked.
- They'll have sex only with the lights out.
- They draw the line at positions and practices that they feel call too much attention to parts of their body they don't like: their breasts, backside, genitals, thighs.

Look at that list again: breasts, backside, genitals, thighs. All the fun parts of you are pretty much off-limits for adoring—every womanly detail he loves, every extra curve that makes a woman a woman. And yet, because these parts of most women's bodies don't match those of the liposuctioned movie stars or anorexic, barely breathing dolls in fashion magazines, or the nubile porn-film ideal set by women with money for daily personal trainers and private carb-conscious chefs, women inflict on themselves a form of self-loathing. It's tragic, it's rampant, and it's much too big a problem for me to pretend that I can offer any easy solutions. So let me offer three thoughts that I have voiced to many female clients over the years, to help them get a better sense of how their dislike of their own bodies may be putting a damper on their sex lives, and how to keep these issues under slightly better control—although it is never easy.

• Those legs and that butt you may think are ugly have carried you through your life so far, and have never failed you. Those breasts have turned a head or two, even if you want them bigger, smaller, higher, or lower. AAA cup or DDD cup, size 6 or size 16, you're healthy.

• Trust me on this: What a woman may consider ten or twenty distasteful pounds of extra flesh her spouse may genuinely see as a very welcoming additional roundness and softness to her curves. (There are exceptions, of course—Harry, the husband in Chapter 6 who told his wife how much her weight gain turned him off, is one. But in general, this is often true. Women don't believe it, but it is.) Or what she believes are unacceptably small breasts, he may see as exactly the right size: just enough to cup in the palms of his hands. What men like most is to feel that the woman they are with likes, even loves, her body—wants to touch it as much as he does. Even if you have to pretend that you love your body, do so, and see where it takes you. This leads me to my next point.

• Resist the urge to call attention to your Buddha pooch in anything but the most positive way. Don't ask if you look fat. Don't ask him if your breasts are big or pert enough for him. Don't point to another woman's breasts and ask if he prefers them to yours. Don't ask him if he wants you to get plastic surgery to look younger or fitter. In other words, don't put yourself down this way in front of your spouse. Because here's the thing: Your husband, like most husbands, will probably be oblivious to your so-called flaws until *you* start harping on them and on him. "You don't see this? How could you not see this? Look at this!" He has probably never thought of you as fat, or small breasted, or getting jowly. The body that you threw at him so sexily when you met is what he remembers and is probably the way he sees you now. And if a woman continues to tell her husband that the wife he has now is too fat, droopy, or jowly, over and over again, he'll start seeing her that way. He'll notice what she tells him to notice. Instead, I recommend giving your breasts pet names—Fabulous 1 and Fabulous 2 or Thelma and Louise or Lewis and Clark (then put him on the expedition). Twirl your skirt up as you pass him in the hall. Grab his hand and put it where the sun don't shine. Invite him to lick you all over. Or do your own wild thing.

Isn't it time you took back your sexual power and used it for "yes, but on my terms tonight, honey" instead of "no, honey, not tonight"?

5. Is it time to consult an updated sex manual? Say that the next time your boiler breaks, you decide to fix it yourself. After a few unsuccessful attempts, however, you decide to go online to educate yourself about possible solutions, or you decide to stop by the hardware store to pick up a manual.

If the efforts you've made to improve your relationship's heating system don't seem to be working, it might be time to update your sex education. Could it be time for you and your spouse to pick up a new manual for your eroticism?

If so, you don't have to go to a bookstore wearing fake Groucho Marx glasses. Most every mall and the outskirts of nearly every town has a store like that with much more than books. Let no sex-toy store or erotic-video emporium go unnoticed. Check your Yellow Pages. Let your fingers do the walking.

But for the slightly faint of heart, you can do all your browsing and shopping and idea gathering from your home computer. Luckily, the range and quality of adult films, toys, books, and other products aimed at couples interested in spicing up their sex life has improved tremendously since *Debbie Does Dallas*, where the women took off their shirts and put on their shirts over and over again. Just a Google away, couples can find everything from erotic films geared for women and men (there's actually some seduction and foreplay before the hunk nails the hottie to the wall) to sex toys made of recycled plastics so couples can increase sexual pleasure and support a greener planet at the same time. Here are a few websites you might want to visit:

• Gamesforloving.com. This site offers sexy computer games designed to be played in bed. You can customize the games to fit your tastes. These games might especially appeal to the partner who has difficulty tearing himself away from the computer at night.

• Flirtcatalog.com. If you like the idea of dressing up in costumes or sexy outfits and accessorizing them with the right gloves, shoes, and, well, whatever comes to mind, browse this website. Pirate outfits are available, but you may have to look elsewhere for a toy parrot.

• Royalle.com. Candida Royalle, a former porn star and all-around smart cookie, went into business with Femme Productions to produce erotic films that appeal to women. This site also has links to other sites offering women-friendly toys and products.

• Goodvibes.com. This site offers adult toys, movies, books, and other paraphernalia that you've probably never seen before and will leave you amazed (and possibly delighted) that somebody actually dreamed them up.

• Tantra.com. Learn the Eastern secrets of longer lasting, more exciting, and more invigorating sex, and become a more spiritual being!

• Secretsinlace.com. A great source of sexy lingerie for ladies of all shapes and sizes. Check out the thigh-high stockings.

By the way, please browse these sites as close to a warm, flat surface as possible, so you and your spouse can tumble into bed or fall to the floor right there if the mood strikes—because just looking at some of these sites can be a turn-on.

Finally, remember this: All stages of love and marriage have their tests and challenges. But the consensus among long-married couples is that if you can hang in through the "devaluation" stage and the particular challenges of raising a family, sex, like love itself, will get better with time: more powerful, more intimate, more delicious. If you think sex was good when the two of you first fell in love, just wait. More than a few sex therapists I know swear that they had their best sex by far after they were fifty. The best is yet to come.

CHAPTER 8

Could Your Communication System Use an Upgrade?

How to Reduce Overload, Avoid Blown Fuses, and Prevent Frayed Wires from Setting the House on Fire

In the previous chapter, I discussed how spouses can improve their sex life only if they are both willing to take responsibility for their own sexual pleasure *and* share their needs and desires with each other. And they can do that only if they are able to communicate clearly, calmly, kindly, and lovingly, and without fear, anxiety, or shame. A husband's and wife's ability to communicate effectively with each other—to talk productively with the goal of listening, being understood, and understanding—powers not only their ability to enjoy good sex, but most every other aspect of marriage as well, much the way electricity powers most systems and appliances in a house. When the wiring frays, fires can start. When fuses blow, rooms go dark. And when this system shuts down entirely, most of the others do, too.

In Parts 1 and 2, I reviewed a number of ways for spouses to communicate more effectively, including, among other techniques, alerting your partner when he or she does something that hurts you; asking for what you want, not what you don't want; responding with curiosity rather than defensiveness when your partner says something that unsettles you; asking questions (and never assuming); and sticking to the issue at hand.

All of these strategies help to reduce tension and conflict and increase trust and emotional well-being in marriage. But it can be hard for spouses to have the clearheadedness and discipline to remember and employ them during times of high stress. In this chapter, I'll introduce some additional overall strategies and techniques that can have the same safety- and security-enhancing effect on a marriage that a general electrical upgrade can have on the wiring system in a house. Spouses don't have to stop and think clearly or do anything specific for these strategies to kick in during times of high stress. Once developed and "installed" in a relationship, they do their job automatically. They're just there.

One of the biggest communication malfunctions I see between spouses in my practice is fear of anger: fear of expressing their own anger, and fear of being exposed to their partner's. Both husbands and wives—though more often wives—may be afraid to acknowledge anger even to themselves, much less to anyone else. As women, we've been raised to keep the harmony and be "nice" (even though the older we get, the more we understand how overrated "nice" can be). Husbands and wives—though more often husbands—also sometimes worry that their anger is too powerful, and that if they let it out even a little, like the miseries released from Pandora's box, it will get out of control.

I try to help spouses grasp the distinction between *feeling* anger— a natural, useful, and even healthy signal that something seems wrong—and *expressing* anger in marriage-damaging ways. All human beings get angry. Anger, sadness, and other so-called negative emotions serve a positive function in marriage and life. They inform the person who feels them that something needs attention, adjustment, repair. It's when a significant issue is *not* verbally expressed but buried beneath the surface, like too much voltage running through a frayed wire, that real problems occur—something blows or bursts into flame. And usually, no one is more startled at the strength of the anger than the person who experiences it. Many husbands and wives have told me they often are shocked by how angry they can get and how fast rage can overcome them.

When stored anger does erupt, couples usually default, almost instantaneously, into what could be called their "signature fight." This is the fight spouses have over and over and over, without ever coming to any satisfying resolution or lasting agreement. It repeats itself every time the wires get crossed, and nothing ever changes. Every couple has a signature fight, either partner can kick it off, and both partners are usually 100 percent sure that it's always the other who starts it: She flipped out because he was stonewalling because she glared at him because he gave her that sneer because she got testy because he got surly because she flipped out because he was stonewalling . . .

These fights differ from the "toxic" fights I discussed in Chapter 6 because in toxic fights, the pattern is for spouses to keep upping the ante—trying to hit back harder than their partner hit them, to top each other, and hurt each other more. In signature fights, couples don't escalate as much as they simply keep going around in the same vicious, dizzying circle—around and around and around until one or the other explodes and walks out. These fights often leave spouses standing aghast in the wreckage after the explosion: How could everything change so quickly? How could they go from feeling love and affection to hating each other's guts so fast?

I'll answer that question in a bit. First, though, be assured that these fights, shocking and hurtful as they can be, are not signs that the marriage is over—unless you leave them untended. They're actually signs that a couple is still deeply engaged by each other and want more from each other. Most serious signature fights occur, in fact, when spouses are wrestling with major marital decisions or marital transitions: buying or selling a house, starting or expanding a family, relocating, quitting or accepting a job, changing careers, deciding how to care for an elderly parent, and so on. This makes sense, as big decisions make for big changes, which make for big stress—even when the changes are desirable. The more stress partners are under, however, the greater the chances of making marital communication missteps that result in blown fuses or worse.

Homeowners seldom welcome the idea of having to do an electrical upgrade on a house. Breaking through walls, replacing wiring, replastering, cleaning up—and the expense! But when a trustworthy inspector or electrician says, "You need to do this," smart homeowners listen. Because what's the alternative? Never mind. They don't even want to think about that. So they do the work, and after it's done, when the mess is cleaned up and the bill is paid (or at least being paid) and they can walk from room to room in their house, knowing they can switch on anything without worrying about overtaxing the wiring, that's when they heave a well-earned sigh of relief. They can now feel confident that the electrical wiring in their home is safe, reliable, and more than able to meet their needs. When spouses upgrade the communication system in their marriage, they earn the right to feel that same sense of satisfaction, security, and confidence in their ability to meet whatever challenges life may throw at their marriage.

Upgrade Your Marital Communication System in Four Simple Steps

In Parts 1 and 2, you assembled some of the tools and skills you need to improve your marital communication system and got rid of others that are wrong for the job. Now it's time to put these tools to use, and to conduct an overall upgrade. Making the following three deceptively simple changes (remember, simple doesn't always mean easy!) can increase your capacity to handle anger and arguments so markedly that, short of a direct lightning strike, you'll never have to worry about system overload and blowups again.

1. Ground your system. You probably plug your home computer into a power strip that also functions as a surge protector—a mechanism that catches spikes and surges in electrical voltage and channels them into a grounded wire, where they can dissipate harmlessly instead of frying the electronic brains of your machine. These surge protectors tend to work so well that homeowners don't even know when spikes or surges occur. They come and they go, passing through the grounded wire without causing a flicker in a light. Couples can prevent surges in stress from frying their marital communication system by grounding that system, too.

I mentioned earlier that I'd explain the dynamics of marital fights that often leave spouses confused and aghast that they could flip from love to hate so rapidly. Here's how it frequently goes: Let's say that a husband is wrestling with a surge in stress or anger—the equivalent of an electrical surge or spike in his personal wiring system. The wife picks up on signs that something is troubling her husband (most wives do), but instead of checking in with him to *find out* what's going on, she guesses, or assumes she knows, or decides she doesn't *want* to know. She gets anxious or frightened or defensive or angry. Now she's wrestling with a stress surge in her own personal wiring system. In moments, milliseconds usually, with one cockeyed look at each other, sparks start flying and they both kick into signature-fight reaction mode. Here's how this dynamic played out for a couple I counseled:

Troy, the former editor of a business magazine that ceased publication, had been a reluctant but good-sport stay-at-home dad for eight months when he and his wife, Alana, came to see me. Alana is an officer at a financial investment firm who travels a lot on business. Troy enjoys being the primary caretaker for their eleven-month-old son, Harry—most of the time. But it isn't lost on him that he and his wife have switched traditional roles and that the work he's now doing isn't considered nearly as sexy or glamorous as the work he did before. He can be a little sensitive on these points, especially when he has been home conversing in baby-speak and wiping Harry's little behind all day while his wife has been off playing master of the financial universe. Just as women who drop out of the workforce to raise kids hunger for adult company and like to know their husbands still find them attractive, Troy often hungered to have a grown-up conversation with Alana and needed to know she still found him hunk-worthy, too.

Most of the time, Alana's genuine attraction to both her husband's mind and body was quite evident. But one early afternoon last January they hit a glitch. Alana was away on business. Troy didn't expect her home until late. Instead, she walked through the door at two PM in the middle of a very bad day for Troy. The neighbor who was supposed to watch Harry for a while so Troy could run to the supermarket had not shown up; Harry had been particularly cranky from the moment he opened his eyes; and Troy hadn't even taken a shower. The house was a mess, Troy was a mess, Harry was a mess, there was no food in the fridge—and Alana arrived home early! Instead of the warm embrace she usually got, Troy handed her Harry and walked away. He was too stressed, embarrassed, and angry with himself that he'd let things get so out of control and that she had walked in on him in the midst of such chaos. He was angry over their reversal of roles, and sorry that he'd agreed to this arrangement in the first place. By the look on Alana's face, it was clear to Troy that Alana was disgusted by him.

Alana, meanwhile, had returned from her trip early because she had screwed up royally. The new client she had gone to woo had decided against signing with her company when she refused to shorten the term of the contract, and her boss was livid. She wanted to unburden herself to Troy while he held her and told her it would all get worked out. She wanted nothing more than his hugs and soothing. When he *didn't* take her in his arms and say the words she wanted to hear, she felt hurt. By the look on Troy's face, it was clear to Alana that Troy sensed that she had screwed up, and he wouldn't be surprised to learn her boss was furious with her. After all, hadn't Troy told her to talk to her boss before taking that hard line with the client? It was written all over his face.

If Alana had asked Troy why he seemed so testy, he would have told her that at that moment he felt like an incompetent slob who couldn't stand himself, so how could she? If Troy had asked Alana why she seemed upset, she would have told him she felt like a total failure who couldn't stand herself, and hoped he'd talk her out of it. But he didn't ask, and she didn't ask. Instead, because they didn't want to fight in front of little Harry, they hardly spoke for the rest of the night. If Troy and Alana had simply known how to ground their relationship with a marriage-counseling technique called "the check-in," all those hurt feelings might have been avoided. The check-in is an exercise that many marriage counselors teach spouses and encourage them to practice daily to prevent stress and pressure from building up between them, and to release the stresses that do. The principal rules of the check-in are simple:

Rule 1: Never assume you know what your partner is thinking or feeling. Always ask. (I mentioned this in Chapter 5, but it bears repeating here.)

Rule 2: Don't wait until you see signs of trouble to initiate a check-in with your partner. Do it regularly.

Rule 3: If it looks like your partner needs to unload, let him vent to you for fifteen minutes without you making a single interruption, verbal or nonverbal (more on this below).

Rule 4: When those fifteen minutes are up, you, as the listener, are not allowed to respond to what your spouse said.

Rule 5: If you also need to vent or if your spouse says something during his or her venting session that you feel a genuine need to respond to, you can't—at that time. However, after a break of several hours—or, even better, overnight— it will be your turn.

Couples are often surprised at the power of the check-in exercise to calm their nerves. I have found that what makes it powerful as a long-term relationship tool is that it literally forces partners to slow down. The talker knows she won't be interrupted, so there's no rush. The listener can't talk, so he can't get too invested in feeling defensive and thinking about how to respond. This exercise also forces the partner who is venting to find words for what he or she is thinking and feeling, which has the same effect as counting to ten or taking three slow, deep breaths. It has a calming effect that smooths out emotional surges and spikes and reduces stress on a couple's marital communication system. One of the biggest tools for improving a relationship in general is slowing down reaction time, as this vastly helps to avoid hurtful mistakes.

If either Alana or Troy had requested a check-in that January day, the tight-lipped evening that followed, and the ensuing fight based on completely misreading each other, might have been avoided. Alana could have asked to vent to Troy, and he could have said, as he often did when Alana was troubled, "Big Poppa's here. Talk to me." And then he could have given her fifteen minutes to talk—to whine, rant, complain, cry, feel sorry for herself, even be angry at him for the mess in the house—as he listened sympathetically without interrupting. (This fifteen-minute time limit is very important. As I explained in Chapter 4, men do much better at this kind of thing if they know ahead of time how long they're in for.) When Alana's fifteen minutes were up, Troy's silent, respectful listening would have helped her reduce her stress, helped him clarify his misperceptions about what she was thinking and feeling, given him useful information about how best he could help soothe her, and given her time to compose herself. Troy could have then asked for his turn as well, and experienced many of the same benefits.

I almost forgot—there's one final rule about check-ins:

Rule 6: If a partner needs a venting session, he or she can ask for it and the other has to say yes. But the partner who asks has to wait until the Super Bowl or cable rebroadcast of *Love Actually* is over!

2. Replace your two-way bulbs with three-ways. Standard lightbulbs have only two settings: on and off. Couples who come in for counseling often discover that their approach to problem-solving has only two settings, too: his way or her way; what he wants or what she wants; what's good for him or what's good for her. Three-way bulbs allow for much more choice and flexibility in lighting effects in a home: soft and low, medium and serviceable, high and bright. Three-way thinking in marriage allows partners more problem-solving flexibility, too. They no longer think only in terms of what's good for one or the other. They learn to make decisions on the basis of what's good for him *and* what's good for her *and* what's good for their relationship. When spouses switch to three-way thinking, problems no longer appear so stark. They begin to see that there's no such thing as "his screw-up" or "her fault." There is only "our problem" that "we" need to try to solve for the sake of "our marriage." The relationship becomes a third entity, like a child that needs to be nourished and cared for in order to grow. Spouses move from taking two individual positions on issues to taking one position as a couple.

Here's an example of how three-way thinking can work. Ron's widowed mother, who lives alone in another state, phones Ron and his wife, Cindy, at least once a day—often more. She calls early in the morning as they're rushing to get themselves and their eight-year-old daughter, Jenny, out the door. She calls late in the evening as they're getting ready for bed. She peppers them with questions ranging from the inane to the intrusive: What are they having for breakfast? Are they saving enough for retirement? Are they thinking of having another baby? What are they having for dinner? Have they decided when they're coming to visit for Christmas? Isn't it a shame about that poor movie star who can't hold on to a man?

No conversation lasts less than fifteen minutes, and Ron's mom always wants to talk to both of them—and little Jenny if she isn't already in bed. When husband and wife finally do get off the phone, Cindy hisses at Ron, "Can you *puh-lease* tell her not to call so much?" to which Ron replies through gritted teeth, "Hey, be my guest."

As long as Cindy and Ron maintain their adversarial positions regarding their "mom" problem, they will not be able to solve it. They'll just keep swatting it back and forth like a tennis ball: "She's your mom. *You* handle her." "Hey, if she makes you so crazy, *you* handle her." If they could stand together in a couple position and see the "mom" problem as a couple problem, the whole tenor of their conversations about it would change. Instead of swatting it back and forth, they might ask:

- How can *we* discuss this without fighting?
- How can *we* talk to your mother about this without hurting her feelings too much?
- Which of *us* would do a better job talking to her?
- Should *we* start letting her calls go to voice mail sometimes instead of always answering?
- Should *we* take turns calling her back and giving each other breaks from having to get on the phone?

When viewed and discussed from a couple position, the problem becomes less divisive because partners know they are working together in a spirit of mutual affection and regard to solve it. (In addition, to whatever degree Cindy may also feel that her mother-in-law's intrusive calls put her in a position of having to compete for her husband's attention, the reassuring "we-ness" of trying to resolve their "mom" problem together eliminates those anxieties and frees her to be more supportive of her mate.)

However, even with the best of intentions to solve problems in a civil, respectful, "couple problem" way, the process will not always go smoothly. Sometimes a husband's and wife's earlier life experiences are so different and the gaps in the way they interpret and react to problems and challenges are so vast that finding a course of action acceptable to both of them can seem impossible: "You think we should do *what*?" Here's another example from my practice, about a couple, Rachel and Michael, who found themselves facing this kind of seemingly unbridgeable divide during Thanksgiving dinner last year with Rachel's parents.

Michael knew all about Rachel's history of being emotionally abused by her father while she was growing up, as her frightened immigrant mother stood by. Or, at least, he thought he did. It was all ancient history now, Rachel had assured him. Her father was who he was. So was her mother. Her father wasn't going to change. Her mother had done the best she could. Therapy had helped Rachel put it all in the past. It wasn't easy for Michael to understand, but maintaining a relationship with them now that they were older meant enough to Rachel for her to let the past go. Michael didn't like Rachel's dad. Truth be told, he thought her dad was an insufferable jerk, but for Rachel's sake Michael maintained a cordial if chilly relationship with him. Or, at least, he managed to until last Thanksgiving, when, during dinner at her parents' house, Rachel, who has always struggled with her weight, reached for a piece of pumpkin pie, and her father leaped. "Fatty, fatty, fatty!" he cackled, pointing a finger at her. "Sure, have another piece of pie. Have two! Hell, have the whole pie! At your weight, what difference will it make?" Michael was aghast. Rachel squeezed his hand hard as a signal not to respond and just kept eating her pie. Her mother looked down at her hands and said nothing. When Rachel's father couldn't get a rise out of either of the women at the table, he turned to Michael, his eyes glittering like hard coals. "You too, Michael!" he said, waving at the pie. "Go ahead! Eat up! You're getting heftier too, eh? That's the way it works, isn't it?" And then he threw back his head and laughed.

Michael pushed back his chair, took Rachel by the arm, and led her into the kitchen. "We're leaving," he said.

Rachel shook her head. "No, Michael, it's okay. Let's go in another room and watch television. Just ignore him."

Ignore him! Was she joking?

No, she wasn't. What Michael couldn't understand, because he hadn't survived what Rachel had survived, was that, at this point, Rachel was deadened to her father's onslaughts. Her shield went up as soon as he opened his mouth, walling out his taunts and her mother's passivity, and walling in her emotional response until he had spent himself. Whatever kinds of problems her mother had, Rachel was not going to abandon her, on this or any day. So Rachel shut down her ears when her father opened his mouth and was thus able to maintain her connection with her mother.

Rachel also knew, as Michael could not, that her father's taunting was just the tip of his potential cruelty, and that any spark of a response from her would boomerang back on her mother later. Thus, challenges from Michael along the lines of "Are you telling me you think this is okay?" or "Don't you see what he's doing?" were not helpful. Even if Michael had never seen so shocking a family interaction in his life, and even if he had had vast experience dealing with other bullies, he needed to defer to his wife when she told him, "Let's just get through this."

That does not mean, though, that Michael needed to completely suppress and deny his own feelings and reactions. In this case, he couldn't. Afraid he would explode if he remained in her parents' house, he said to Rachel, "Look, you stay if you want, but I can't." This upset Rachel terribly, although she understood. She suggested he take a long walk and pick her up in thirty minutes. For his wife's sake, and what she claimed was a deeper understanding of the issues, Michael agreed. He went for a walk, returned half an hour later, entered and stayed in the house just long enough to collect his wife, and kept silent about Rachel's dad.

When they described the incident to me later and Michael expressed concern for his wife's welfare, they were able, by thinking in threes, to work on this problem to a point where Rachel, who would have preferred to just go home and forget that the incident ever happened, found a better way to take care of herself at future visits—by making them short and by agreeing never to commit to having a meal there again. At Michael's suggestion, she also decided to start inviting her mother out with her during the day—just the two of them, alone.

There is almost no thought, worry, feeling, or need that spouses can't handle in a better fashion using the rule of three: Is it good for him? Is it good for her? Is it good for their relationship?

Take a moment right now to think of a problem or conflict that is plaguing your marriage. How would shifting from individual positions to the couple position change your and your spouse's perspectives? If you held your separate agendas up to the light of thinking in threes, would either agenda hold up? If not, can they be blended? If not, can you toss both out and come up with something totally new?

Practicing this problem-solving approach leads couples along a path to greater intimacy, because it requires them to think more carefully about why they feel the way they do about something and why they like an idea or don't, and then spurs them to find a way to communicate these thoughts and feelings to their partner. Committing to thinking in threes and acting in threes is one way partners work toward knowing and loving each other better.

3. Install power-savers. Cost-conscious homeowners who want to reduce their electrical bills are usually careful to check the energy-efficiency rating on appliances when they buy a new air-conditioner or refrigerator, for example. Many also look for appliances that come with power-saver modes built into them. Almost all computers have them now: Walk away from the computer and it powers down and goes to sleep; touch a key and it powers back up. Some homeowners install other power-saving devices that put all the electrical appliances and devices in their home on an energy-saving diet, feeding them only as much power as they need to operate and no more. Why use more and *pay* for more if you don't have to?

Spouses can save energy and reduce power struggles in marriage by powering down when they are tussling with an issue. If it's not critical that a conflict be settled instantly (and it seldom is), the wiser course of action is to take a step back, shrug a good-natured shrug, and say: "Okay, you say 'po-tah-to' and I say 'po-tay-to.' How about we just leave it at that for now?" The truth is, many sources of marital friction and conflict cannot be resolved to both partners' satisfaction; the best course of action may be to recognize an argument as futile, and move on.

Don't get me wrong: Agreeing to disagree is not often easy, particularly when the issue at hand is more weighty than, say, a disagreement about whether *Titanic* is as great a movie as *Gone with the*

Wind. Josh and Lila, a couple I counseled last year, for example, fought for more than a month over whether Lila should accept a promotion to become head buyer for a chain of women's clothing stores—a position she had been inching her way up to all her working life, but which would involve a lot of travel, including regular trips to Europe. Josh had supported Lila's dream when it had been just the two of them. But they had a seven-year-old son and a five-year-old daughter now, and Josh's job as vice president of a men's clothing manufacturing firm already kept him at the office later than he and Lila liked. How would they arrange childcare when she had to travel? How would Lila hold up her end of things at home? How would the kids be affected? It was one thing for her to dream about flying off to Europe before they started a family, but things were different now. If Lila took the job, it would affect everyone's life.

Lila, of course, could not believe that Josh would want to try to stop her from taking the job she had always dreamed of having. She felt stunned, injured, betrayed. She thought Josh was being selfish. Josh thought *she* was being selfish. She didn't care.

"I am not going to pass up this opportunity, Josh," Lila told him.

"You take the job, Lila, and, I'm telling you, you're going to regret it."

"Is that a threat?"

"No, it's not a threat! I'm just telling you how I feel. I think you *will* regret it. You'll miss the kids. You'll be stressed out all the time. We'll never see each other. I think we'll all regret it. You won't get back these years with the kids."

"You think I don't know that? But you know how much I've always wanted to do this. I'm going to love it so much I won't even mind the stress. And, if we play it right, our tuition worries are over."

Josh threw up his hands. "Okay, but don't say I didn't warn you."

So Lila took the job. And all the positive things she thought would follow did follow, and all the negative things Josh thought would happen happened, too. She had less time for the family. He had more housework. They had more money. She had more job satisfaction and more stress. She missed the kids. He missed her. The kids missed her. And so forth. The arguments started afresh.

"I am tired of doing almost all the cooking and eating dinner alone with the kids almost every night because you can't get home at a decent hour, Lila," Josh told his wife when she walked in the door at nine PM one night, three weeks into the job.

"Well, you're going to like this even less," Lila said tentatively, bracing for her husband's reaction. "I have to go to Paris this weekend."

That's when they came to see me.

"She has to leave the job. We can't work this out," Josh complained during their second session.

"Maybe, for now, it would be better if you stopped trying," I suggested.

"What do you mean?" Josh asked.

"Table it. Give yourselves time to become more familiar with your new lives. Set a date when you'll bring it up again: in one month, three months, six months—you decide. But, in that time, you'll both focus on trying to help each other adjust and make the best of things. Because this is all new and you're both too stressed to make a clean decision about it." They had already been doing some daily check-ins and scheduled venting sessions. "Keep those up," I said. "But stop trying to solve things now. Give it as much tabling time as you want, and when that time is done, you'll know more, and you'll be able to have a much more productive conversation." I reminded them that whatever length of time they picked, they had to promise not to mention their problems during that period. Not even once, if they could help it.

Josh and Lila agreed to give this a shot, because anything seemed better than the constant bickering they had fallen into. They decided on three months, and they decided to write out a five-step plan and put it in their night-table drawer. Here it is:

Josh and Lila's 3-Month Plan for Not Solving Problems

- We agree not to try to solve our work-family problems for three months.
- We agree that three months from today, on September 14, we will make time after dinner to talk privately and discuss these problems again.
- Until then, we agree that we will not refer to these problems. We will check in with each other three times a week, but we will limit all venting to daily events.
- During this period of no discussion, we will focus on making the best of our situation and exploring new ways to think about and deal with the challenges it presents.
- Three months from now, on September 14, we will compare notes on what we have learned and discuss ways to make our work and family life more satisfying.

Josh and Lila stuck to their agreement, even enjoying a laugh or two when one person had to clamp a hand playfully over the mouth of the other. In taking this issue off the table, the time actually flew by. By knowing they couldn't discuss things, the tensions lessened.

When they had their powwow three months later, many aspects of their situation looked different. Josh had found that he enjoyed spending more time with the kids, even though they left him exhausted. "I realize now that I hardly knew my kids before," he said. "They are such cool kids." Josh and Lila also reported a positive upswing in their sex life. "We have so much less time together now," said Lila. "I guess you could say that when we are together, we make the most of it." Both of them enjoyed being able to afford extra luxuries, such as season tickets to the ballet, and they were both excited about an upcoming family skiing vacation in Colorado, which they never could have afforded before.

But there were still frictions and conflicts. During one session, they got into a heated discussion about housework. Josh argued strongly that he simply could not be expected to keep shouldering so much of the load himself. He needed more help. Lila argued just as strongly that she couldn't be expected to do an equal or even bigger share if she was never there and that, given how seldom she was home now, she did *not* want to spend that time doing laundry. Back and forth they went until Lila finally said, "Look, how about we just hire someone to come in once a week. We can afford it, don't you think?" Josh mulled for a moment. "You know what?" he said, smiling at Lila. "You're right." He stuck out his hand, and Lila shook it. "We did it!" they said simultaneously, smiling at each other and shaking again.

What had Josh and Lila done that made them so happy? When they left my office and went back to their daily lives, Josh would still feel overworked and exhausted more days than not, and Lila would still have little time with her family. But they felt pleased that, when they had problems to work through, they could expect to be successful at it—together. They could live with their differences in a renewed atmosphere of trust—and with a cleaning lady. Once a husband and wife know how to do that, everything else is a piece of cake.

They had also learned to be gentle and generous with each other in ways that could only bode well for them going forward. Lila had sat listening with genuine empathy, for example, when Josh had talked about desperately needing help with the housework, without ever once hinting at what every working wife and mother in the world could have said: "Hey, buddy. Welcome to the club." But then, Lila didn't have to, because Josh was there first. "You know, I owe you an apology, Lila," he had said during that same session. "All those years when you were working and doing most of the housework and childcare, I didn't have the first clue what it took for you to keep everything running the way you did."

I cannot emphasize this enough: Success in marital problem solving has little to do with actually *finding* a solution to a problem. It has everything to do with how spouses conduct themselves and treat each other 1.) as they search for a solution and 2.) when a solution can't be found. In the final analysis, the most important question spouses can ask and answer in order to keep their marriage strong is: How can we live with problems we can't solve?

Making these simple upgrades in your marital communication system will not eliminate *all* ugly explosions and blow-ups. Sometimes something between spouses just snaps, like lightning striking a house, and the air between them goes electric and they *want* to fight and *want* to hurt and *want* to be nasty—and when they do, no one and nothing is going to get in their way. Now, however, you will have so many more options, you don't have to go there. Meanwhile, making these general, safety-enhancing improvements in your marital communication system will let you rest easier and make you far less susceptible to fire and weather changes. Even when the lightning is flashing directly overhead, you can sleep soundly in each other's arms.

CHAPTER 9

Getting to Know and Love the Nooks and Crannies

Foolproof Ways to Increase Intimacy and Connectedness

To take good care of a house, a homeowner must be aware of and perform all types of upkeep and maintenance regularly: Once a month, the wide-plank floor in the dining room needs waxing to maintain its shine; that third spindle in the curving banister needs to be checked every few weeks, because it has a way of coming loose. Upkeep and maintenance aren't always fun. The work can be annoying, tedious, and expensive. But even as homeowners whine about seeding the lawn or putting towels against the old leaky window during a storm, most will also admit that there is a certain ironic amusement that comes with knowing a house well—rolling their eyes as they squeeze the water out of the towels they placed below the window, trudging to the attic together to let the squirrel out yet again. Knowing a home well enough to be on intimate terms with its quirks and foibles is strangely gratifying, partly because you can anticipate problems, and they never let you down.

In a marriage, the usefulness of knowing each other's quirks and foibles comes up all the time—in the many ways spouses step in to protect and pinch-hit for each other. There is immense pleasure in feeling that your partner knows you well enough to spare you a phone call from your sister that he knows you don't want to take (without asking) or to throw something together for dinner because he knows you are too tired to cook (without asking). It's a deeply affirming feeling when the two of you are in sync. Yet, no matter what you already know about each other, there is always more to learn, and the continued exploration of each other can be very rewarding—and fun. Even when it isn't, when you learn something about your spouse you'd rather not know, staying close to each other is about finding ways to affirm, reassure, respect, and honor your relationship every single day (without sounding like a Stepford wife).

When two people fall for each other, accolades pour out of their mouths without a second thought. They can't say enough wonderful things about each other, sometimes driving those around them nuts. Each couple has stories about their compatible flukes and mutually arresting quirks—and they are very specific and very vocal. It's not just that they both love movies—it's that they both love sci-fi movies . . . made before 1960 . . . with spaceships constructed from tinfoil. Each coincidence, even the smallest of synchronicities and factoids, takes on the monumental meaning that the two were meant for each other.

At some point after marrying, however, as I discussed in Chapter 1, spouses start having less-than-positive learning experiences about each other as well: He promised his mom that she could come live with them when her health starts failing. She's smoking again—he can smell it on her breath. He refuses to throw out the Sunday paper until he's read it all, so the papers are in a pile in the corner, dating back to an article about the invention of the DVD player. She said she was a great cook, and she is—of meat loaf and absolutely nothing else.

Around this time, after these revelations have been occurring for a while, partners can be tempted to pull back and stop talking to each other openly, for fear that one more negative discovery will be more than they (or their marriage) can take. What couples at this stage often fail to realize, however, is that, along with these unpleasant realities, there are countless other *positive* things about their partner still to be learned; more of the wonderful tidbits that drew them together in the first place. And the more of these positive revelations they collect, the closer they feel to each other. The more exploring spouses do, the more deeply known and loved each feels by the other—and the harder it gets to devalue each other because of the bad stuff.

There's no denying that the ongoing work of exploring your partner is, in fact, *work*. But it can be enjoyable work. And this work is essential for building and maintaining intimacy and connection, which, as you know from Chapter 3, make up so much of your relationship's foundation. In this chapter, I'll offer some foolproof ways to increase these important components of your marriage.

Grab That Flashlight Again—It's Time to Go Exploring:

Four Ways to Get to Know Your Partner Better

What positive or interesting things have you learned about your partner lately? What have you discovered about him recently that totally surprised you or reminded you of why you fell in love? Have you been doing your check-ins, as I suggested in Chapter 8? Here's a quick test to evaluate how much time you've put in to "getting to know" your partner lately:

- Do you know what made him happiest during the past week?
- Do you know what's worrying him most right now?
- Do you know how he's feeling about the two of you right now?
- If a friend of his asked him how *you're* doing, do you know what he'd say?
- Do you know the one thing you did in the past week that made him happiest? Not what *you think* made him happiest—what *he would say* made him happiest?
- Do you know the one thing you did this week that upset him the most? Again, not what *you think* upset him most—what *he would say*?

If you can't answer these questions about what's going on with your husband and marriage right now—and please don't feel bad if you can't; many spouses can't—then you probably aren't paying enough attention to each other. And beyond these fairly basic questions, there is likely a lot going on inside both of your heads and hearts that's worth knowing and that the other partner isn't aware of. Some of researcher John Gottman's books on marriage contain extensive quizzes and questionnaires to help partners get reacquainted—to pick up where they left off when their marriage hit the devaluation stage and to restart the process of exploring each other's inner lives. In that spirit, here are some exercises you might want to consider trying.

1. Introduce yourself to the ghosts in the attic. All houses that aren't newly built come with histories—sometimes long and fascinating ones. Spouses come with histories, too. Partners often start out wanting to know everything about each other's histories, but then real life starts soaking up more and more of their time and attention, and the inclinations they may once have had to explore each other's past takes a backseat to keeping up with daily demands. The more spouses do know about each other's backgrounds, though, the better they can understand each other and put some of each other's annoying idiosyncrasies (we all have them) in context.

One of the nicest ways to spark your partner's enthusiasm for talking about his life is to literally take a trip through his old neighborhood. I have heard countless stories of people who light up while pointing out their old school and the spot where they had their first kiss. If you can't do that, perhaps you can initiate a conversation during a long car ride or over a glass of wine in your den. But remember: The nature of men may mean that the request "Tell me more about your childhood" will elicit the response "Nothing to tell." So be specific and ask questions such as:

- What did your childhood bedroom look like? Did you hang stuff on the bedroom walls?
- Which of your friends got you in the most trouble in school? What was the worst thing the two of you did that you got caught for? What's the worst thing you did that you got away with?
- What was your favorite sport in high school? What was your best single play? What's the one play you flubbed that you'll never forget? Was there any sport you wanted to try out for but didn't?
- Were you ever bullied? By whom? Did you ever get into a fistfight? How old were you? Who did you fight with? How did it end?

- Who was the first girl you ever had a crush on? How old were you? Did she like you? Who was the first girl you ever kissed? How old were you when you learned about sex? Who told you?
- What's the best birthday present your parents ever gave you? What was the worst? What's the present you wanted that you never got?
- What's the most wonderful thing your mother and father ever said to you? What's the most hurtful thing your mother and father ever said?

You get the idea. And, if still pressed, you can always go at this with an old family photo album in hand. Besides helping you learn who everyone is and making you laugh at your partner's mullet, the album may allow you to glean insight by observing family positioning and facial expressions—how close or far away people stood from each other, whether they were smiling. Family photos can speak volumes if you look closely and think about the relationships (as much as if not more than about the outdated clothing).

2. Stay attuned to (and respect) your partner's needs and wants. My dear friend, the late director and playwright Betsy Carpenter, once told me about an award-winning play she directed called *Swimming in the Shallows* by Adam Bock. In it, one of the characters, Barbara, visits a monastery in Thailand where the monks are allowed only eight possessions. Barbara decides she wants to live like these monks and begins tossing out possessions while her husband, Bob, who likes buying and owning things, keeps buying her more. In a review of a later staging of the play, *New York Times* critic Neil Genzlinger took issue with this spiritual-emotional divide between Barb and Bob. "Must all middle-aged couples grow apart?" he asked. "Aren't there at least a few who actually grow closer as the years pass?" Yes, there are. There are many, actually. You can increase the chances that you and your husband will be one of them by doing everything you can to keep each other aware of your current wants and needs—and tolerating each other's occasionally strange stages of life. Like Bob might have done when Barbara went through her minimalist phase. Like Helen, a client of mine, did when her husband, Kyle, decided to start shaving his full head of black hair for about a year. Or like another another client, Dom, did when his wife, Melanie, decided to wear only red for a year.

As for the subplot of Bock's play, it does suggest some interesting questions for you and your partner to try out on each other:

- Of all the material things you possess right now, if you could keep only eight of them, which would they be? Why?
- Of all the material possessions that were once yours but no longer are, which one do you wish you still had, and why?
- Of all the modern conveniences of life, which would be hardest and which would be easiest to give up?
- If your house was burning and you could only grab one thing on the way out, what would it be?
- Are a pair of shoes one thing or two things?

3. Purge the pipes. Homeowners know that, every now and then, it's good to go around the house testing seldom-used spigots in the laundry room, basement, or garage to make sure they're still working, that they haven't rusted shut, that the water pressure is adequate, and that the water coming through them is clean. The ten questions listed below have been known to have a similar effect on people. They seem mundane, but it's amazing what people reveal about themselves when they answer them. This questionnaire was first developed by a French television talk show host named Bernard Pivot, who asked them of each of his guests on a show called *Bouillon de Culture*. James Lipton, who interviews well-known actors and actresses in front of an audience of acting students on an American TV show, *Inside the Actor's Studio*, now ends each of his interviews by posing these same questions to each of his famous guests. Ask your husband:

- What is your favorite word?
- What is your least favorite word?
- What turns you on creatively, spiritually, or emotionally?
- What turns you off?
- What is your favorite curse word?
- What sound or noise do you love?
- What sound or noise do you hate?
- What profession other than your own would you like to attempt?
- What profession would you not like to do?
- If heaven exists, what would you like to hear God say when you arrive at the Pearly Gates?

Spouses may think they know how their partner will answer many of these questions. Frequently, though, they discover they're wrong—except for each other's favorite curse word, which they've usually heard more than enough of. Try this: Instead of just answering these questions for yourself, begin by answering for your partner and vice versa. Compare your answers with what your partner thought you would have answered (and vice versa). Any surprises?

I have done this in my practice, giving couples these ten questions and asking them to answer for each other rather than themselves.

Marty was sure he knew what job Darshana would want, other than the one she had as a teacher. She always talked about medicine and read medical journals. So, logically, when he answered for her, he answered that she'd be a doctor. But he was wrong. To his surprise, she said that if she could be anything, she'd want to be a marine biologist, studying dolphins in the wild. "I read those journals," she explained, "because they are full of diseases I want to make sure I don't have and don't get and know how to recognize if I do get them—not because I want to be a doctor." On the other hand, in the past, when Alice told Pat that she wished she had pursued ballet, Pat thought Alice was mostly joking. When they did this exercise together, however, Pat realized that Alice meant what she said. She had actually studied ballet as a child, but had had to quit when her parents fell on hard times. Armed with this new information, several weeks later Pat surprised Alice with a gift of ten ballet lessons at the local Y. Alice was so deeply moved and felt so deeply loved and understood by Pat's gesture that all she could do at first was cry. When your partner shares dreams and disappointments with you and vice versa, you can not only join in making the other's dreams come true, but also feel closer to each other by knowing that you understand and care about each other's secret desires.

Taking Care of a Spouse Is Like Taking Care of a House—Four Essential Rituals to Boost Intimacy and Connectedness

A colleague of mine named Blanche told me recently that when she was growing up outside Chicago, her family made a weekly Saturday ritual of cleaning their two-bedroom apartment. She and her sisters—and their parents, if they weren't working Saturdays—would start with the bathroom and front-hall closet, then clean the bedrooms, then tackle the kitchen and front room. Blanche can still remember the different polishes and cleansers they used; nicking her knuckles on burners as she scrubbed the kitchen stove; polishing every knickknack on her mother's prized shadow box. She didn't always enjoy this Saturday ritual, especially after she hit puberty. But she hardly recalls that now. What she remembers today are the laughs, jokes, and arguments that sometimes broke out among her and her sisters on cleaning day: "It's your turn to clean the bathroom." "No, it's yours." How much more fun the chores were when their mother was working and their dad was home heading the crew. "We'll just give everything a spit and a polish," he'd say with a wink. She'd never heard that expression before. "And then, when we were through, my sisters and I would take our Saturday-night baths while my dad went to get pizza," Blanche said. "Then we'd all sit around, my sisters and me in our pajamas, eating pizza and watching TV." Blanche had no way of knowing it would turn out this way then, she said, but, she admits, "That Saturday ritual is one of my fondest memories now."

The rituals of maintaining and nurturing your connection with your spouse—the daily, weekly, and monthly tasks, chores, and responsibilities spouses take on and fulfill through high points and low, good times and bad, to care for each other and their relationship—have the same long-term, marriage-strengthening, intimacy-enhancing effect. Soon after a couple marries, they begin cementing their relationship through the conscious application of rituals and routines such as: using grandma's good china on the most special occasions and carefully washing it and putting it back in the china cabinet together afterward; making each other breakfast in bed on Sundays; always making their own birthday cards for each other; making his mom's brisket recipe (and avoiding her mom's ambrosia recipe concocted from Cool Whip and canned peaches). Over time, spouses with a strong desire to increase intimacy and connectedness develop all kinds of personal rituals for staying connected: for example, having private pet names for each other or each other's body parts. (Winston Churchill called his wife, Clementine, his "cat," and she called him her "pug.") Their secret ways of making each other laugh, getting each other's attention, or signaling support and affection across a crowded room can be endearing.

As you and your spouse grow old together, the ordinary, day-to-day ways in which you honor and care for each other can be counted on to strengthen and maintain the intimacy and connection you share. If you suspect that you and your husband could honor and care for each other *more* on a daily basis, here are four effective ways to do to so:

1. Develop good daily maintenance habits. Even in the busiest households, caring and showing respect for a home usually includes a host of small daily acts, such as wiping down a kitchen table after breakfast and gathering up any bowls or glasses left in the living room from late snacks the night before. These daily acts of attention and care become a kind of unwritten code of household etiquette that parents also teach their children: "Yes, you can go to the mall, after you make your bed."

In marriage, spouses often start out observing a similar code of good marriage-maintenance etiquette—always kissing good-bye and hello, for example. Sometimes, though, as life gets busier and more stressful, couples let these good habits slip. Taken one by one, they can seem like such little things. Yet, every one of these small daily acts of love, respect, attention, and affection plays its part in maintaining intimacy and connectedness in marriage. And every one skipped, dropped, or forgotten weakens it just a little bit. Here are some marriage-maintenance habits that should not be forgotten:

- Kiss good-bye. Don't just call out "I'm going!" or "See you later!" from another room. Make a point of reuniting before one of you leaves.
- Hang up the phone when your partner comes home. Let your partner feel that he is more important than talking to your girlfriend.
- Remember that showing appreciation is not optional. Find something to appreciate—and do it every day.
- Find out at least one thing about how your partner's day went each day.
- Touch often and with great tenderness.

2. Make regular inspections. Although you've worked at learning to think in terms of "we," the two of you can't do *everything* together. One partner pays the bills, another handles travel arrangements, and so forth. However, have the two of you found the best person for each job? Knowing each other's quirks means accepting that Sally may get overwhelmed and neglect to pay the phone bill for a few months and Frank may not realize it until they get a disconnection notice, or that Joe may forget to book the plane tickets to go visit Rosa's mom for Christmas until it's too late to get a flight. Spouses get busy, forget, procrastinate—usually in the same ways over and over. To help your marriage run most efficiently, a simple thirty-minute meeting every other week can be set up to review what needs attention, what slipped through the cracks, what needs repair. (When spouses commit to holding these meetings, they both agree to be accountable for their given tasks—which, in effect, greatly minimizes potential nagging!)

- "Did you remember to call the airline? If this is a bad week for you, I can do it."
- "Do we have any bills that need paying before our next meeting?"
- "Johnny seems to be really struggling with math this year. I was thinking maybe we should consider getting him a tutor."
- "Kathy and Dave Marshall want to know if we're free for dinner on the eighteenth. I said I'd have to check. I know you're not crazy about Dave, but Kathy's been such a good friend to me lately. What do you think?"
- "There's a crack in the bathroom ceiling I'm a little worried about. It might just be the paint, but I'm not sure. Would you mind taking a look at it?"

You and your spouse may have to force yourselves to stick to the meeting schedule for the first few months. But it's worth doing, even if it's always a drag and you always have to force yourselves to find the time. These thirty minutes will mean fewer screw-ups, fewer fights, and a lot less yelling in the house. The team gets things done that the individual might have flubbed up.

I also encourage couples to use this meeting time to make a plan for that old cliché "the date night." I know what it sounds like, but almost every long-term happily married couple swears by the importance of getting away alone together regularly—even if, sometimes, all they can manage is a picnic in the backyard. The point is to be alone together and enjoy each other. So, while a dinner out is optimal, you can settle for tacos on the front porch. Just don't let the custom, an important part of maintaining intimacy in your marriage, fall by the wayside.

3. Don't skimp on repairs. By now you know that when you see a crack in the wall, you better find out what's going on behind the crack before you cover it up and call it fixed, because simple cosmetic repairs are too risky. Cosmetic repairs between you and your spouse can have the same outcome—things look all right for a while, but the crack is actually getting deeper. As I pointed out in Chapter 3, an empty "I'm sorry" is one of those cosmetic repairs— especially when it is followed by an explanation such as "I didn't do it on purpose" or "How was I supposed to know you're so sensitive?" There are two exercises for apologies that I now regularly teach to clients because so many couples have told me how much these exercises increase their feelings of intimacy and connectedness. And, like many of the others described above, they can actually be surprisingly fun.

Exercise #1: Name your evil ways.

Here's the rule: No putting a scratch in the dining room table or a stain in the hall carpet and just keeping quiet and hoping your spouse won't notice. If you did it, you admit it. You name your evil ways. The late Don Jackson, one of the founders in the fields of family and interactional therapy (therapy that focuses on how people relate and interact) was the first to develop this structured concept, in which partners fully and formally admit their marital trespasses to each other. He suggested that when things are calm between spouses they should sit facing each other and take turns listing the ways they each contribute to tensions and strains. A husband might say, for example:

- "I criticized your haircut last week."
- "I didn't call you to say I'd be late, like I said I would."
- "I yelled at you when you told me you were upset."
- "These are my evil ways."

The wife might then respond:

- "I blew up at you yesterday in front of the children."
- "I refused to talk to you after you came home late."
- "I left the kitchen a mess on purpose so you'd have to clean it up."
- "These are my evil ways."

Couples often end up turning this exercise into something playful as a wife confesses to eating the last piece of pie that she swore she didn't eat or a husband apologizes for making funny faces behind her mother's back the last time they visited. You may come away feeling that genuine confession and remorse are cleansing to the soul, but don't be surprised if the two of you dissolve in giggling instead. This exercise works best, however, when spouses are dealing with minor transgressions, such as a husband carelessly leaving a toilet seat in the upright position for a wife to discover while doing a midnight landing and other comparatively trivial but nonetheless hurtful and annoying day-to-day mishaps. The next exercise can be better applied to repairing more serious hurts.

Exercise #2: Maintain the 5 to 1 ratio of repair.

After interviewing, videotaping, and observing thousands of married couples, John Gottman concluded that in long-lasting, happy marriages, couples tend to engage in at least five positive interactions for each negative one. Letting that positive-to-negative ratio slip below 5 to 1, he found, is a fairly good predictor of divorce. Put another way, this suggests that when one spouse wounds the other, it usually takes a *minimum* of five genuine repair efforts—five sincere acts of generosity, thoughtfulness and kindness—to erase the hurt and set the relationship right again.

Approached with the right attitude, this can be a rewarding and enjoyable process for both spouses—a chance for partners to show each other that they're not only sensitive, mature, and caring enough to be aware of, confess to, and feel bad about hurting each other, but that they're also attentive, playful, and imaginative enough to come up with some pretty original and effective ways to set things right. Most couples have certain ritualistic ways of making up after fighting. I know one husband who always brings his wife a bouquet of thirteen pink roses. Corny maybe, but it works. I know a wife who gets up early and brings her husband breakfast in bed. Also a cliché, perhaps, but in their case, it also works. Another wife comes up behind her husband as he's sitting on the sofa and starts giving him a shoulder massage. Another husband runs a bath for his wife. As soon as she hears the water running, she begins to feel better. Many spouses, of course, also have "makeup sex." Nothing new there, either—but plenty of fun for all involved.

Think about some of the special ways that you and your husband try to soothe each other's hurt feelings and restore warmth and connectedness after you've had an argument. The next time one of you wounds the other, up the number of loving overtures you make. Even if the first one seems hugely successful (that would probably be makeup sex), enforce a discipline of consciously adding another kind word or gesture, and another, and another, and *another*, until you've tallied up a total of five. Use your wit, be novel—the sillier or more surprisingly original the better.

If you: Ridicule him for not being able to figure out how to put together the "easy assembly" desk you bought at the home furnishings store.

Then you: 1. Say you're sorry. 2. Treat him to a sexual favor of his choice. 3. Locate the sunglasses he misplaced two weeks ago and gave up hope of ever finding. 4. Make dinner on his night to make it. 5. Throw the dishes on the floor and have makeup sex on the table.

If you: Say something nasty about his mother.

Then you: 1. Say you're sorry. 2. Treat him to a sexual favor of his choice. 3. Invite his parents to dinner. 4. Make him breakfast in bed. 5. Throw the dishes on the floor and have makeup sex.

If you: Compare him negatively to another man who is financially more successful.

Then you. 1. Say you're sorry. 2. Treat him to the sexual favor of his choice. 3. Give him a foot rub. 4. Buy him that new biography of Jefferson he's been dying to read. 5. Throw the biography of Jefferson on the floor and have makeup sex.

Think of these acts as investments in the future closeness, stability and happiness of your marriage—because they are.

4. Make your house a home. You've probably had the experience of visiting a home that was so gorgeous, so exquisitely decorated, so perfect in every detail—each book and objet d'art elegantly arranged on the coffee table, every pillow on the sofa plumped and tilted just so—that you found it hard to believe anyone actually lived there and even harder to imagine living there yourself. It wasn't cozy or inviting in that warm, welcoming, broken-in, creaky stair, worn-out carpet, drippy faucet kind of way that makes visitors feel at ease. You want to go for that same warm, welcoming, love-and-fun-come-first quality in your marriage. If the kitchen floor's sticky with spilled cranberry juice after a party, in other words, and your husband's hot to make love, what do you do? That's right. You forget all about the kitchen floor except maybe to make love on it. There are times when the most essential aspect of marital maintenance is to forget about maintenance and simply have fun. Some ideas:

- Transmit messages with Morse code kisses.
- Leave a silly surprise—or even better, an erotic surprise—under your husband's pillow.
- Take him to an amusement park and kiss at the top of the Ferris wheel.
- See which of you can recite a tongue twister five times fast without flubbing it.
- Make Little Eva proud. Do the loco-motion naked.
- Give each other secret Magic Marker tattoos where nobody except the two of you will see them.

Surprises, mischief, laughter, and good sex are the love potions of an enduring marriage—the all-natural energy elixirs, the immune-system boosters, the restorative salves and balms. Consider this: A wealth of studies now indicate that men and women who enjoy close, supportive, and satisfying relationships are less physically reactive to external sources of stress, recover more rapidly from illness, have fewer recurrences of serious health problems such as heart attacks, and heal faster from physical wounds. These are just some of the benefits of a loving, mutually satisfying, long-term relationship.

By this point, if you've been testing and applying the techniques and strategies for marital improvements and repair that I've offered chapter by chapter, with any luck you are feeling more confident about the chances that your own marriage will improve, grow, and mature into one of these precious, health- and intimacy-enhancing, lifelong unions. If so, you have every right to feel "spouse proud." In the next section, I'll help you stand back, admire all the fine work you've accomplished, and set off the work to the best advantage with some final finishing touches.

PART 4

Spouse Proud

CHAPTER 10

Finishing Touches

*Decorating Tips to Give Your Marriage
That Special Glow*

When homeowners complete a major renovation, they tend to feel a yen to give the rooms in their home a fresh look to match the fresh work. Few do-it-yourselfers want to keep their smelly couch, yet they can't afford to throw out their old furniture and buy new. Instead, they need to cast a new eye on the same old possessions, to sift through carefully and decide what still fits and which items no longer have the same charm and value or don't serve the same function they once did. Other pieces may simply need a little love to massage them back into their former glory—placing them in a different spot in the house or installing better lighting can make what you thought was a tired old table look surprisingly stunning. This is also the stage in a renovation when homeowners happily begin unpacking and arranging cherished belongings—framed family photos, that silver vase they bought in Arizona, all the finishing touches that make a house a home.

You've now reached the "finishing touches" stage in your relationship renovation as well. You've gotten rid of harmful tools and
behaviors, and you have an appreciation for the new skills you've
learned. Since you appraised your marriage back in Chapter 2,
you've worked hard to repair and improve it, and you now have a
realistic sense of the rigors of mature love. It's time to put those final,
loving touches on your marriage—time to reposition and polish
up a few last marital habits and ways of interacting with your
partner to display the true worth of your spouse and marriage to
their best advantage.

This stage of the relationship-renovation process engages all
of your senses and sensibilities: touch, smell, taste, vision, hearing.
Reaching out to stroke your partner while waiting with him in a
doctor's reception area can actually lower his blood pressure.
Nuzzling your face in his neck and breathing in that smell you
noticed the first time you did so can trigger the same feeling now
as it did then—that you belong together. Something as simple as
giving him a bite of your salmon from your fork affirms the same
symbolic promise you made to each other at your wedding reception, when you fed each other cake. It says that you will always
nourish each other. Making an effort to please each other visually—
you by wearing the sweater with the dropped shoulder that you
know he likes to see you in; him by putting on those low-slung
boxers he knows you think make him look sexy—help to keep
the heat between you turned up high. And, of course, what you say
to each other and how you say it—how you soothe each other,
boost each other's spirits, root for each other and support each
other's dreams, keeping your voice and tone soft, low-pitched,
and warm as opposed to harsh, loud, strangled, and squeaky—all
this makes you both feel more respected, appreciated, and cared

for, emotionally safe and deeply loved. When spouses reach this stage of marriage renovation, they begin integrating these and other finishing touches into their daily married life rather than using and displaying them only on special occasions—because they understand that their relationship *is* their special occasion, every single day.

It's time now for you to dust off, polish up, and display some of those finishing touches that you've been holding in reserve for use only when the two of you are in public, perhaps, or on special marriage occasions, and making them a more integral part of your daily married life. Decorators rely on certain tricks for making a house look expertly finished for years to come without breaking a homeowner's budget. Here are three of their most effective techniques, adapted for relationships.

1. Steal from the best in the business. Top decorators go to open houses, museum and furniture shows, and read decorator and architecture and design magazines as part of their routine. Everywhere they go, they're always on the lookout for new ideas—ideas they can steal from the best. Why not?

The marital equivalent of copying great ideas from other sources is to pay close attention to other happily married couples, and to copy what you see and hear them doing. You've probably been observing happy couples for years without realizing how your observations can serve you well, because you may have been looking at these couples with the wrong attitude. In the past, you may have said, "Why can't we be like that?" or "Why aren't we that happy?" Now, instead, you will see that if you copy some of their behaviors, adapting them so that they fit your personal style, you *can* be like that and you *can* be as happy. Those couples haven't made a better match. They simply treat each other better—as the two of you are currently doing.

When you see those couples now, ask yourself:

- What are the first things I notice about a happy couple?
- How many of these things are also a part of my marriage?
- What stands out as positive behaviors and traits that are *not* currently a part of my marriage?
- What ideas do I have for incorporating these positive behaviors into my own marriage? How do I think my partner will respond?

Copying and repeating the positive behaviors you see in other couples can bring more good feelings into your relationship as you continue improving it. As explained in Chapter 3, a school of therapy called cognitive therapy operates on the premise that people's thoughts, beliefs, and behaviors *create* their feelings.

Maria and Miguel are a perfect example of the powerful effect that copying good behaviors can have on a couple's relationship. They entered therapy and worked very hard to learn constructive fighting skills, as they had both come into the marriage from unhappy families whose fighting repertoire included behaviors such as "yell as loud as you can," "stomp out," "drink heavily," and "threaten divorce." One afternoon, Maria called to cancel an appointment, explaining that her father had died suddenly of a heart attack, and she and Miguel needed to fly home to Puerto Rico that evening. When we met again, several weeks later, Maria recounted the event, as well as a significant change that had occurred between her and Miguel as a result of it.

When Maria arrived at the funeral home, all her parents' friends whom she had known as a little girl were there. There was this one couple her parents' age—the Lopezes—that she found remarkable. They looked fantastic—as if they hadn't aged a bit in the twenty years since she last had seen them. She remembered them from her childhood, especially the way they looked at each other and touched each other, always holding hands. It had had a huge impact on her as a child, and she still remembered wondering why her parents couldn't seem to behave the same way. Even at the funeral, there they were, looking at each other and touching each other in exactly the way she remembered them—still so much in love.

Miguel had to fly home the day after the funeral for work, but Maria decided to stay on longer to help her mother for a while. During that time the Lopezes brought over a meal, and Maria had more time to watch them together. At one point, Mrs. Lopez was washing dishes when Mr. Lopez walked over and brought her hand cream to apply when she was finished. Maria made a joke about it and then asked Mrs. Lopez, "Seriously, how do you two do it?" Mrs. Lopez answered simply, "We've worked hard at it every day for thirty-seven years." At which point Mr. Lopez laughed and said, "And we don't scratch the gnat bites."

Maria thought about what he meant—all those times she had picked on little things that were better left alone. The loss of her father whom she deeply loved, the work she had done in her couples therapy, the wish to make the most of her own marriage—thoughts of these things were with her when she returned home, and led her to an important decision: She would begin to behave with Miguel the way the Lopezes did—so seamlessly—with each other. From the moment Miguel picked her up at the airport, Maria was decidedly more demonstrative with him. She began to groom him, running her hands through his hair, and grabbing his arm on the street. For a split second he didn't know how to respond, but then he squeezed her hand, and she was surprised at the effect it had on her. She also began working hard at biting her tongue and letting small irritations pass rather than commenting to Miguel each and every time he did something to annoy or displease her. She began working at "not scratching the gnat bites," in other words. It didn't take long for Miguel to notice this, and for Maria to notice how quickly her new verbal restraint had the effect of reducing some of Miguel's usual edginess at home. The more she touched him and the less she picked at him, the more he responded and the closer to him she felt. Before long, neither of them was conscious of these new behaviors—it was just the way they were with each other, and it came more naturally than they'd ever dreamed it would.

2. Adjust the lighting. If you're a film buff or theater fan, you understand the impact lighting design can have on the overall effect of a movie or play. Cineastes can talk for hours about how this or that scene in a film was lit. People who see favorite actors or actresses in real life are often struck by how different they look in person than they do on screen—thanks in part to makeup, of course, but thanks also to lighting. In the world of Broadway theater, lighting design is honored each year with a Tony—the theatrical equivalent of an Oscar. Sophisticated home decorators also know how beautiful almost anyone or anything can be made to look in the right lighting—subdued lights and candlelight for example—and how harsh and ugly even the most beautiful person or possession can appear when the lighting is wrong.

In marriage, lighting is also crucial. Spouses can view each other through the equivalent of the harsh glare of a fluorescent light—the kind of light police officers sit suspects under when they're grilling them in the back room. Or they can bathe each other in softer, warmer, more flattering light—light that makes them each look and feel more like ageless movie stars, like Grace Kelly and Cary Grant. When partners view each other through the soft, warm, flattering light of respect, understanding, and love, their best features are played up and their harsh edges are softened. But the difference flattering lighting can make doesn't stop there. Because when spouses view each other through softer lighting, they fill up with softer, more loving thoughts about each other. Kindness, generosity, and compassion don't have to be forced. They come naturally—as does treating each other with goodwill.

Goodwill comes after the rose-colored glasses are long gone—when you know the truth about mature love and you have the guts to pursue it and stick with it anyway. When, day after day, you make the choice to be with someone who has almost everything you want, *and an awful lot you don't*. Goodwill is the ability to focus on your spouse's strengths, to see him in a positive light. When you exercise goodwill, you:

- Assume that your spouse is in the marriage for the long run and that his annoying idiosyncrasies are not a comment on or threat to his commitment to you.
- Give him the benefit of the doubt first and always when you're tempted to question his motives or behavior.
- Ask questions about things he says or does that you don't understand rather than make accusations or harbor secret suspicions.

- Accentuate the positive, applaud his accomplishments, and appreciate his strengths.
- Ignore his occasional bad moods and let his occasional sniping or snarling roll off your back when you know he's feeling stressed and the bad behavior will pass.
- Say "ouch" to alert him when he crosses the line from harmless snarling to hurtful behavior—and stop there as long as he gets the message and backs off.
- Forgive and forget quickly and laugh things off easily.

Extending goodwill can be as simple and difficult in the beginning as stopping yourself from thoughtlessly swiping at your partner over a mundane event or chore (don't scratch the gnat bites) and taking the high road of mindful requests and gratitude when he responds. Try this:

If he: Takes out the trash.

Don't say: "I was wondering when you'd finally get to that."

Do say: "I see you took out the trash. Thanks."

Work up to: "Thanks for taking out the trash, sweetie."

If he: Takes your car in for a tune-up.

Don't say: "I'll bet you forgot to get the inspection sticker renewed, right?"

Do say: "The car rides so much smoother now. Thanks for taking it in."

Work up to: Thanking him again the next day ("You know, that was really nice of you") or praising him in front of other people

("Notice how much smoother the car is running, kids? That's because your dad . . .")

You may be thinking, "I shouldn't have to thank him for taking out the trash—what with all I do around here." And you may be right. But how has being right helped your relationship in the past?

Everyone wants to be thanked, appreciated, and praised. Attack and criticize your spouse, tell him he has failed or disappointed you and you leave him nowhere to go with that information except to feel bad about himself—and ultimately about you for making him feel bad. Tell him what he does that pleases and delights you, and you give him the gift of helping him figure out what makes you happy. Remember: This is not manipulation—you're not trying to sell him swampland in Florida. What it is is communication on a higher plane. A plane that most spouses aspire to, but one that's not always easy to reach—especially during times of stress.

A woman named Margie came to see me, for example, without her husband, Hal, when their marriage hit a big stress bump. She would have preferred to have him accompany her, but Hal came from a family that didn't believe in therapy, so that was that. Margie was a head nurse at a local hospital. Hal headed an airline maintenance crew at a local airport. Usually, he was the first out of the house in the morning and the first back at the end of the day. Recently, though, Margie had been told that, due to a staff shortage at the hospital, she would have to extend her hours. Now she was the first one out in the morning and the last one home at night. Given this change, she had felt it was reasonable to ask Hal to take over some of the tasks she had always handled before: making their bed, for example—because, after all, he was the last one out of it now and it meant so much to her to come home to a well-made bed; dropping off their son and daughter at school in the morning (formerly Margie's job), for another example; and making dinner for the kids two evenings a week—not every evening, just two.

"He agreed to do it, but he's doing a lousy job," Margie said during a session, venting to the right person at least: me, not Hal. "He doesn't really make the bed. He just kind of straightens it. And on the nights he's supposed to make dinner? Please. Pizza. He serves the kids pizza—that's his idea of dinner. And he tries to tell me all four food groups are represented. Plus he walks around the house grumbling all the time about everything he has to do now. Excuse me, but I never complained even when I was up to my elbows in diapers." Margie thought Hal was acting like a spoiled child. "I don't want to get into a fight every evening, but on the other hand I don't want to silently fume every night over what a half-assed job he's doing, either." What she wanted, wisely, but didn't know how to accomplish, was a solution that would allow her and Hal to feel good about themselves and each other.

Bed making, meal prep, and grumbling were Margie's three legitimate gripes against her husband. And Margie *did* have a right to feel resentful. But how to handle it and keep the peace, as the situation wasn't likely to change in the near future? Margie first had to ask herself some questions:

- Would venting her anger at Hal help her get what she wanted from him? The answer seemed obvious: no.
- Would she feel better if she vented? In the short term, yes, she said. But in the long term, probably not.
- Would criticizing Hal's bed-making skills motivate him to do it better? Unlikely.

- Would he grumble less if she told him it was annoying? Unclear. Maybe, maybe not.
- Would he start cooking real meals for the kids if she put the screws to him? He might try, but they'd probably be awful because he was a really bad cook.

At that point I asked Margie: "Did you marry Hal because he was a good housekeeper?" She laughed at that. "No!" she said. "Hal lived like a slug in a swamp when I first met him. And the only thing he knew how to cook was chicken with ketchup."

"So he's never been a cook or housekeeper," I said.

"No," Margie said.

"And you knew that when you married him."

"Yes."

"And you married him anyway."

"Right."

"And you married him because . . .?"

That stopped her. "I married him because," she said softly leaning back against the couch, repeating my prompt, and then she talked for the next twenty minutes about just a few of the many things that she felt made her husband such a wonderful man: his rough childhood as the eldest of six children whose father abandoned the family when Hal was ten; the way he'd worked three jobs at once to put himself through airline mechanic school; how smart and funny and kind he was; what a hard worker, loyal friend, and loving husband he was; what a big heart he had; how much the kids adored him . . .

I nodded. Margie had switched from viewing her husband through the harsh glare of a fluorescent light to viewing him through the softer light of generosity without missing a beat.

"Okay, then," I said. "You didn't marry Martha Stewart, and you're obviously very aware of your husband's good qualities. You also seem happier talking about that."

"Oh, I don't want Hal to become Martha Stewart," Margie said. "I just want him to put more care into cooking and bed making. Cooking, especially, I guess, because he's feeding our children. And I'd like him to care more about how much it upsets me when he does a lazy job."

"That's clear enough," I said. "So you'd like him to acknowledge that he's slacking off, care about how it makes you feel, and maybe do a better job. Now, can you think of ways to accomplish these goals—or at least enough of them to satisfy you?"

Margie turned the ideas around in her head. Okay, she said finally. Maybe expecting Hal to make the bed to her liking was expecting too much, she admitted. "I have all these pillows on the bed arranged a certain way," she said.

"How many pillows?" I asked.

Margie blushed. "Well . . . fifteen."

"That's a lot of pillows."

Margie weighed out her feelings about her cozy bed. "If he could get the bedspread right," she said, "I could put most of the pillows on a shelf in the linen closet. I really only ever use two anyway."

"Have you shown him how to do the bedspread?" I asked.

"No," she said. "I could do that, too."

"That might help."

"I suppose I could adjust it when I get home, also."

"And what would you say to him about that?"

Margie said. "I could just do it. I don't have to say anything. I don't really care about that nearly as much as I do about the kids' meals. That's much more important."

"Okay, so what about the meals? You said he's a terrible cook."

"He is, but he's not stupid," she said. "He knows how to read a cookbook. He can follow a simple recipe."

"Does he have a cookbook?"

"No," Margie said. "I should get him one."

"Will he use a cookbook?"

"No. You're right. I'll ask him to get veggie pizza or find a couple of decent frozen meals."

"And his grumbling? Can you live with that? I mean, doesn't he have a right to grumble?"

"If we could reach an agreement on these other two things, I might not mind it so much. Maybe I'll just try to ignore it."

Feeling calmer about the possibility of resolving their differences without rancor, Margie went home and presented her ideas to Hal that same night. To her relief and surprise, he liked all of them, and things took a rapid turn for the better. Margie got rid of the pillows (Hal kissed her hand when she did, which made her laugh) and showed Hal how to work the bedspread. When he got it wrong the next three days in a row, she quietly adjusted it. Perhaps as a show of gratitude for not being criticized, Hal quietly paid attention to how she adjusted it and within a week he was doing it right. In return, as a show of gratitude for this clear indication that he cared about pleasing her, Margie thanked him profusely every time she came home to a perfectly made bed: "Oh, honey, *thank* you." (She also found herself feeling more sexual more often.) As for Hal's grumbling, yes, he still grumbled. However, now that she was happier with the solutions she and Hal had worked out, she actually found his grumbling kind of sweet. One day she walked up to him, put her arms around his neck, and said, "I know, it sucks." He broke out in a big smile, as if that was all he ever wanted.

How had Margie worked this seemingly amazing transformation in the mood of her relationship? First, like any sophisticated decorator, she switched to softer, warmer, more flattering lighting. She also made some other subtle but key adjustments. Among other things, Margie:

- Resisted the urge to attack or fight with her husband
- Put the issues that were upsetting her in perspective by viewing them against the larger backdrop of her husband's many good qualities
- Recognized that problems are problems—not character flaws
- Practiced three-way thinking—what's good for him, what's good for her, what's good for their relationship—rather than insisting on having everything her way
- Decided which issues mattered more to her and which mattered less, and focused on resolving the important ones and letting the unimportant ones go

Then Margie:

- Took responsibility for resolving her unhappiness rather than simply stewing about it
- Spoke to her husband directly and calmly
- Helped him fill in gaps in his knowledge and skills in a nonjudgmental way
- Quietly brought things up to the standard she needed to be content without making her husband feel bad that he hadn't met those standards
- Thanked and praised him when he did meet her standards
- Allowed him his emotional responses—if he needed to grumble, he needed to grumble

- Didn't take his emotional responses personally
- Looked for the humor in the situation and lightened the mood in her marriage even more by finding ways to lift her husband's mood, too

Finally, here are three other things Margie told me she began reminding herself of when she felt the good lighting of mature love for her husband starting to get out of adjustment and her goodwill starting to slip:

- They're his children, too.
- It's his house, too.
- He has as much say in how we raise our family and run our home as I do. It's *not* all up to me.

That didn't stop all their arguments or eliminate all their tensions, she said. But it did greatly reduce them by illuminating disagreements in a way that made it harder for her to see issues in stark black and white.

Wise, I told her. You could say that when it comes to how Margie chose to view her husband and her marriage, she became an artist of light.

3. Display your precious mementos. One of the most enjoyable aspects of visiting a friend's home or having a friend over for the first time is the opportunity it provides for two people to get to know each other better, by sharing stories about precious possessions: "This was my grandmother's chest. It used to sit at the foot of her bed in her farmhouse in Kentucky." "This is a picture of my brother Arnold as a college radical. Can you believe that hair?" "See this silly little two-dollar stuffed bear? My husband must have spent twenty-five bucks trying to win it for me at a ring-toss concession at a county fair the day he proposed."

Most homeowners enjoy sharing stories about their photographs and possessions with other people (sometimes too much—we all know the joke about the couple with the endless slides of Hawaii), but that's not the main reason they fill their homes with these treasures. They do it because of the deep pleasure it gives them to be surrounded by these tangible artifacts of who they are, who they've loved, who has come before them, and what will live after them. Such items help create meaning in their lives—the connections to what they've celebrated, what they've mourned, what they've laughed at and triumphed over, what they've lost, what they've survived. Whether it's a shell picked up on a beach vacation or a photo of the great-grandparents, these mementos help give the house its unique character.

Make sure your house and your heart contain the kind of sweet memories that give your marriage meaning. Hopefully, you've displayed photographs taken of the two of you on your wedding day, your honeymoon, or a special vacation or family event, and when you see them, they give you a tingle when you're in the right mood. The photos act as a protective cocoon that reminds you daily of what you've got. Margie told me, for example, that when she felt the light of her feelings toward her husband begin to shift from warm and rosy to cold and harsh, she would pull out a shoebox filled with old snapshots she kept meaning to arrange into scrapbooks, and she would randomly sift through them: There's Hal in the delivery room the day their son was born; he swore he'd faint if he was present at the birth of his first child. There's Hal on the floor of the delivery room. There he is on their honeymoon, falling off a surfboard in the waters off Costa Rica, where he took a surfing lesson to impress her but, try as he might, never did manage to stand up on the board. There he is hugging her mother and planting a wet kiss on the top of her head when she went in for hip-replacement surgery. There he is, glitter all over him, building a model of the universe with their daughter. Margie is smart enough to let the photos do the job she needs them to do when her feelings waver, and the photos still haven't let her down.

During my years of practice, I've been touched and tickled countless times by the ways couples have told me they keep loving memories, and loving feelings, alive. Some tell simple stories, such as trudging through a deep snow for a first date and returning every year to the same restaurant on the same day (then going home and having great sex). Other couples have much more complicated tales. Ted proposed in a paddy wagon when he and Penny got taken into custody after a protest march. Now, every year, they return to the precinct with a gallon of orange juice for the cop who arrested them. Rhodes and Mina skydive on their anniversary. Evan and Mei Ling compose long handwritten letters to each other.

You get the idea. It doesn't matter what spouses do, really, to keep good times and good memories alive. The only thing that matters is that they do it. Being able to access these memories is so central to the health of a marriage that therapists often rely on data from these memories as a diagnostic tool. During a first session the therapist will ask the couple to recount how they met. If the couple tells the story jointly, animatedly, arguing good-naturedly about small details, filling in pieces each feels the other overlooked, going back and forth, that's a good sign. It indicates that, whatever problems they may be struggling with, their loving memories are still strong—and the ratio of positive to negative feelings between them probably remains well above the five-to-one ratio I mentioned in the previous chapter. It also indicates that they can temporarily be distracted from whatever is bugging them at the moment.

If, on the other hand, they can't do that—if, instead, one tells the story of the day they met or the day they married in a detached tone while the other picks at his or her fingers or stares out the window, or if one or both spouses wave off the question with some version of "That was so long ago, who can remember?" or "What does that have to do with anything?" that's not a good sign. It's an indication of a deeper and more troubling disconnect. In my own practice, this stage of disconnect means it is going to be a long journey back to closeness.

Bearing in mind that you and your spouse have made it to this stage in your relationship renovation, however—that you've already done the hard work of drawing yourselves closer to each other—you don't have to worry about that. You are now approaching the beginning of the next and most satisfying stage of your life-long journey with your partner: the pride and appreciation stage.

In the next and last chapter, I'll help you continue to admire the results of all the work you've done to improve your relationship. I'll also help you decide how to handle life's unavoidable but temporary setbacks as well as any lingering urges you may feel to keep making more improvements. Should you give in to them? Resist them? It may surprise you to hear this, but the wiser decision may be to resist them.

CHAPTER 11

There's No Place Like Home

He May Not Be Perfect, but He Is Your Old Spouse

ɪn the preceding chapter, we talked about the many ways that finishing touches and accents can breathe new life and energy into a room or relationship you've renovated and make it even more fabulous—how something as simple as a softer-hued lightbulb or gentler way of viewing your spouse can be magically transformative. It's a great feeling to get excited all over again about a house or relationship you've lived in for years and perhaps taken for granted. What can top that feeling of sitting on your newly reupholstered living room sofa, for example, pleased to know that the hours and hours you've spent getting the look of the room just right has been successful? Ditto for the new rug that brings out the color of the freshly painted walls, the throw on the sofa that completely covers the stain that bothered you all those years, and the plants that make the room even more inviting.

However, even as homeowners indulge in this feeling, gazing around their renovated living room or bedroom or kitchen, admiring all their fine work and perfect finishing touches, inevitably they are going to trip upon some not-so-fine work and not-so-perfect finishing touch. The section of the bedroom wall where the paint is glopped up. The nick in the new kitchen molding. The gap between two squares of the new parquet living room floor that slipped past unnoticed, and now seems glaring. This moment often comes as a blow to do-it-yourselfers. Now, all of a sudden, instead of enjoying everything they've accomplished, all they can think about is this ugly spot, that oversight, and those mistakes. They begin to wonder: What else have I missed? What else got screwed up? What else isn't going to hold up for very long?

In a love renovation as in a home renovation, couples sometimes reach a stage where they run the risk of overlooking or minimizing the very real improvements they have made in their relationship because all they can see is that the relationship still isn't perfect. It's a shame when couples work so hard, and instead of enjoying what they've accomplished, they notice only the work still left to do— those little or not-so-little annoyances and problems they haven't addressed or resolved or learned to live with yet.

If you have come this far in the book, done all the good work, and feel better about your marriage but aren't sure you feel "better enough," consider that you may be experiencing your own version of these "post-renovation blues." In this chapter, I'm going to describe what *to* do and what *not* to do to calm these perfectly predictable twitchy feelings of dissatisfaction and to prevent them from robbing you of the *other* feelings you're entitled to: appreciation for the work you and your spouse have done and pride in the improvements you've made.

Even the Best Do-It-Yourselfers Are Human

Every once in a while, I see stories in the newspaper about a home renovation project gone sour when the house in question turned out to be a real lemon: built on a sinkhole that yawned open and swallowed the house whole, or located across from a high-rise that the home-buyers didn't know would be going up and blocking their ocean view, or positioned down the road from a cow barn that spreads its stink through every room in the house when the wind blows the wrong way. In marriage, too, inevitably there are times when spouses feel that their marriage and their partner is a total lemon. I wish I could promise that now that you've developed your sensitivity, empathy, and compassion for your partner and mastered so many new skills for addressing problems calmly and constructively, these moments will never come again. But the truth is, they will. Not as often as they did before, but they will come.

The late psychoanalyst Emmanuel Ghent once said: "Marriage is about learning to tolerate what you hate most about your partner." Cynical, I know, but there is truth to it. Tolerating what you hate most about your beloved means not just living with the usual aches and pains of a relationship between two caring yet separate individuals, but living with the complete pain in the butt your partner can and will occasionally be—as you will be, too! And when the storms hit, this can certainly seem like a nearly impossible challenge—yet couples do survive these periods, and end up feeling glad they stuck it out. Some of the long-married couples I've talked to say they've learned that when one partner drives the other crazy, it's best to take the same attitude they take when mice get into the basement again or the roof springs another leak: "Well, this sucks. I'm miserable, and I'm probably going to stay miserable for a while. But I'll deal with it, and I'll get through it. I don't have to like it; I just have to do it." What else can they do? As one long-married woman told me, "You learn to live with it because, when you marry, you can't just marry the parts of your spouse that you love. You have to marry the whole person." It's just like buying a house: Homeowners don't just get the splendid kitchen and the cozy fireplace. They get the cramped bedrooms and the wasps' nest in the attic, too.

I would actually go a step further than Dr. Ghent did and point out that marriage isn't only about learning to tolerate the thing you hate most in your partner. It's also about learning to tolerate the things you hate most in yourself. Almost twenty years of practice as a marriage counselor have taught me that when spouses do cave to the impulse to scream or take cheap shots or freeze each other out or slam doors (and all spouses do now and then), they don't especially like themselves much afterward. In fact, the more work they've done to develop more mature ways to deal with stress and problems, the more horrified they are when they slip back into these counterproductive ways. Spouses who learn to pause during times of stress and reflect on how they handled the same aggravating situation in the past and how they felt about it later— remembering how awful they felt the last time they exploded, for example—are better equipped to avoid these slip-ups in the future, at least some of the time. It's the equivalent of remembering the last time they sprinkled poison throughout the basement and felt so bad about killing a mouse that they vowed, "Never again. From now on it's have-a-heart, traps." For spouses, however, the vow might be: "Never again. From now on I leave the room instead of blowing up."

To repeat: All spouses will slip up occasionally—you and your partner included. That's when you will be faced with the challenge of accepting and even forgiving your own weaknesses and flaws. When these times come, it can help to remind yourself that you and your husband are not machines that can be programmed to always respond in a desired way. Rather, you will both often find yourselves engaged in an internal tug-of-war, wanting to win and behave well but sometimes losing out to meaner impulses.

When this happens, you must simply remember to take the appropriate steps to repair any damage as soon as possible. And you can take comfort in the knowledge that you are committed to learning from your mistakes, and that you, like your marriage and your house, are a work in progress.

Every House and Every Marriage Is a Constant Work Site

A woman I counsel named Chandra recently found herself engaged in exactly this kind of struggle with herself: She was angry at her husband, Terry, for dropping the ball when it came to finishing repairs to the guest bathroom after water damage from a burst pipe ruined the walls and floor. Knowing Terry couldn't care less about decorating schemes, Chandra took care of the aesthetic aspects of the job herself—and felt pretty good about herself for doing it with such generosity of spirit. She studied paint chips and tile samples until she was cross-eyed, narrowed down her choices to two possible color schemes, and only then asked Terry for his opinion: Which did he like better, the stone-and-sand scheme or the blue-and-gray? When he said he didn't care, whichever one she liked, she didn't push it or try to engage him in a conversation about it. She made her choice (stone-and-sand), ordered the paint and tiles, and simply asked Terry what would be a good day for the two of them to start pulling up the old tile floor. She was more than ready to assist, but this was where she needed Terry to take the lead. He knew this stuff. She didn't.

"Well, not this week," Terry said, not even looking up from the newspaper he was reading.

"Okay," Chandra said, generously. "How about a week from Saturday? Would that work?"

"Yeah, sure," Terry said, again not even looking up. When the agreed-upon Saturday rolled around, Chandra put on her work clothes and went to get Terry. "I'll be right there," he said. He just wanted to finish a chapter in a Carl Hiaasen novel he was reading first.

"Okay," Chandra said, generously. "Maybe I'll get started."

"Sure," Terry said.

Chandra went to the guest bathroom, got down on her hands and knees, pulled up two loose floor tiles, took one look at the mess underneath and went to find Terry. "Honey, I think you need to take a look at this."

Heaving an irritated sigh, Terry put down his book and followed Chandra into the bathroom. He squatted down and poked at the rotting wood under one of the ripped-up tiles. "Wow, that's pretty bad," he said.

"We should take care of this right away, don't you think?" Chandra said.

"Yeah," Terry said. "We should at least get those old tiles up."

"Can I just keep pulling them up like that?" Chandra asked.

"Sure," Terry said. "Don't see why not."

"And then?" Chandra asked.

"I'll take care of it," Terry said.

So Chandra spent the rest of the day pulling up the old tiles herself. *Okay*, she told herself. *So he won't get started on his part of the project today. That's all right. I'm sure he'll get to it tomorrow.*

But he didn't.

Okay, Chandra thought. *Next weekend for sure.*

Two months later, the tiles were still piled in a corner of the guest bathroom, the ugly, spongy underflooring still exposed—and Chandra, who had been so pleased with her generosity and patience for so long, was starting to lose it. "You know what?" she told me during a session. "I don't think he has any intention of *ever* fixing that floor—which wouldn't be so bad if he would just *admit* it so I could get someone else to do it. But he won't! He just keeps saying, 'I said I'll do it'—and never does. And, now that I think about it, this isn't the first time he's pulled this stunt. There are the shelves he still hasn't hung in the den, and the end table he still hasn't refinished, and the dimmer switches he still hasn't installed in the living room . . ."

Chandra was feeling completely frustrated and getting angrier at Terry with every unfinished project she recalled—and there were many. Now, the repairs that needed to be made weren't just mounting up in Chandra's home. They seemed to be mounting up in her marriage, too. Chandra had gotten to the point most marriages reach every now and then when she was mad as hell and didn't want to take it anymore. What should spouses do when they reach this point? *Shift their focus.*

The Best Decorating Trick of All:

Stop Focusing on Your Partner and Focus on Yourself

In Chapter 10 I mentioned the huge difference lighting can make in the beauty of a room or a relationship. Light either one harshly and even the most beautiful person or possession can look ugly. Light a room or relationship with soft, warm lighting, and everyone and everything in it looks more beautiful. Flaws are minimized. Warts and wrinkles disappear. Decorators are also adept at arranging things in a room to draw people's attention *toward* what they want people to focus on and *away* from what they don't want them to see. If they want to draw attention to a cozy alcove, for example, and away from a room's low ceiling, they might place a low table and small decorative lamp in the alcove to draw people's eyes down to the table and away from the ceiling. Spouses often use some version of this technique in marriage, too. Chandra certainly tried to. No sooner had she finished angrily rattling off her long list of Terry's unfinished projects did she turn right around and try to refocus on all his good qualities and strengths: "But his job is so demanding, it's amazing he has any energy left for anything, really. And then there are his parents, of course. They demand a lot of time and energy from him, now that they're getting older." But hard as she tried to get her mind off the unfinished bathroom floor, she couldn't. "It isn't fair," and "he promised" just kept eating at her, session after session—until Chandra stumbled upon the one refocusing strategy that *almost always* works, even when all the other ones have failed: Stop working on your partner, and, if you have to work on something, work on yourself.

While the torn-apart bathroom sat like a little totem of despair, Chandra got involved in organizing and training for a 10K race to raise money for Habitat for Humanity, one of her favorite organizations. As soon as she started training, she almost forgot about the bathroom and she forgot to be angry at her husband. Instead she talked mainly about how great it felt to be training again, how she'd forgotten how much more energy she had when she was in shape, how excited she was that her company had decided to sponsor the race, and how much money she hoped it would raise. For the next three months, Chandra was so completely engaged with this project on every level—physically, mentally, and emotionally—that she often went entire counseling sessions without mentioning Terry's unfinished home-improvement projects.

The race was a huge success. It raised even more money than Chandra had hoped it would, she ran her best personal time ever, and her boss thanked her publicly at the post-race dinner for organizing such a wonderful event. For the next two weeks, Chandra remained on a high. But then it faded, and with nothing else nearly as exhilarating on her personal horizon, she returned to the issue of the unfinished bathroom, which now took on the grand proportions of:

- an ISSUE
- a power struggle
- the absolute biggest, most pressing problem in Chandra's life and the fall of civilization as she knew it

For three months, Chandra hadn't given the unfinished bathroom floor much more than a passing thought. Now she was sure that, at any moment, the entire bathroom was going to go crashing down into the basement.

And whose fault would it be if it did? Terry's, of course. Now Chandra was angrier than ever—because another three months had gone by and Terry still hadn't done what he had promised to do!

After Chandra vented for a while, I asked her a question. "Chandra, what is it you really want most here? Do you want to get the bathroom fixed? Or do you want to stay angry at Terry? Because if you want the bathroom fixed, you could get it fixed. You could just call a repair person or ask your brother to help you do it. If you'd rather stay angry with Terry, though, you could do that, too."

It was time for Chandra to accept that finishing the bathroom was *her* priority, not her husband's. He wasn't trying to be difficult. He just wasn't doing what she wanted him to do. And Chandra was right: He probably wasn't ever going to get around to it—at least, not in the foreseeable future—no matter how often or in what tone of voice she asked. Chandra needed to decide whether she wanted to live with an unfinished bathroom or get it fixed herself, let her husband off the hook, and get on with her own life.

Chandra didn't answer my question right away. Instead she simply said, "I'm going to have to think about that." And she did, very seriously—because promises were important to her, and she tried hard to keep all of hers. The idea of Terry being a different person with different beliefs about the sanctity of a promise—even one about a bathroom floor—was something she needed to mull over. Two weeks later, she said she had decided to get her brother to help her refinish the bathroom floor. Terry had protested when she (calmly) told him of her decision, so she had said (calmly), "Okay, one week. I'll give you one more week. If you can't get to it by then, I call my brother—deal?" Grudgingly, her husband had agreed.

Two weeks later, when the bathroom was still untouched, Chandra called her brother: "I'll cook you dinner if you'll help me with the bathroom floor." He agreed to come over the following Saturday when Terry would be off running his parents around on errands. "I realized I didn't want to be angry at him," Chandra said. "And I didn't want to embarrass him in front of my brother, either. I just wanted to get the job done." By the time Terry got home that evening, the bathroom floor was finished. Terry said, "Geez, you didn't have to do that. I was just about to get to it." But, underneath that, Terry was so (competitively) inspired (something we so hope for in husbands) that the following weekend he finally hung the shelves in the den, without being asked.

In houses and in relationships, no renovation is ever finished. There are always other projects to tackle, other jobs to do. Sooner or later, most homeowners realize that they have to make peace with these imperfections. Think about it this way: Accepting all the flaws that will never change and the imperfections that no one has the time to get to is a huge relief! One satisfying life moment is cutting that to-do list in half. Perhaps the time has come for you to experience the unbearable lightness of the stop-work order. Because, as Chandra learned:

- You can't bully your partner into being a better partner.
- It's often exactly when you're most frustrated with your partner that you most need to leave him alone.
- It's often exactly when you feel the strongest impulse to dig in and work on your marriage that you most need to leave your marriage alone.
- It's often exactly when you feel most determined to work on your partner and your marriage that the best solution is to *work on yourself*.

If your reaction to this last point is, "But *I'm* not the problem!" all the more reason to leave the problem alone. If the problem has nothing to do with you, if it has only to do with your partner—as Terry's record of never finishing projects had to do only with him—then, chances are, you can't fix it.

One of the most gratifying aspects of the work I see couples in my practice do occurs after I ask dissatisfied spouses: What would you be doing with your time if you weren't spending it focused on your partner? Their first reaction toward me might be annoyance, but after giving this some thought they often are inspired to take on some healthy solo pursuit or activity—boxing or photography or volunteering for Meals on Wheels. It's amazing how suddenly many of their marital complaints drop off their radar screen. P.S.: You don't have to be unhappy to take up something like this. It's also a great way to *stay* happy.

A woman I counseled named Angie complained, for example, that she felt her husband, Ben, had completely lost interest in her since she had become a stay-at-home mom. She needed some attention from him when he came home from work after she'd been home all day with the kids, but it was as if he just couldn't be bothered anymore. She felt hurt and betrayed, and nothing she said to her husband seemed to help. Six months later, she began working part-time as an activities coordinator at a senior center. As soon as she did, everything changed. She realized that it hadn't been Ben who'd lost interest in Angie; it had been *Angie* who had lost interest in Angie. While feeling depressed, she had somehow gotten the idea that Ben was supposed to cheer her up. As soon as she started doing work she enjoyed and began liking herself better, she began liking and treating her husband better, too.

The Paradox of Home Repair and Relationship Repair

Okay, suppose you don't have a charity race or a part-time job to distract you and help you refocus your mind productively instead of getting sucked into a whirlpool of focused frustration with your partner. You will still have to find a way to summon the discipline to change your focus because it is a step toward marital health—and to avoid doing it is a step toward marital decay. Look at it this way: When a top-notch painter, computer-repair person, or electrician is working in your home, you know enough to stand back, right? You wouldn't crowd, annoy, or insult respected professionals by shadowing, questioning, or trying to orchestrate their every move, would you? You would hardly expect them to be able to do their best work if you did that, correct? The same principle applies to continuing to focus on those aspects of your marriage and your partner's personality that are still (and always will be) less than perfect. It's an even bigger problem to magnify these remaining flaws to the point where they become almost the only thing you can see. Most spouses absolutely agree with this, in theory. Yet their actions often belie their beliefs:

• Peggy fell into a habit of following her husband, Jacob, into the bathroom to continue an argument while he was showering, which prompted him to start locking the bathroom door, which prompted her to start standing outside the door shouting at him while he showered, which prompted him to greatly extend the length of his showers.

• Bart almost never calls Lucy from his office during the day when things are going well between them. But if they have a disagreement that isn't completely resolved before they both leave for work in the morning, he makes an annoying and embarrassing pest of himself, phoning her at her office every hour on the hour until Lucy can find time to return his call and assure him that he can relax, she's not angry anymore, everything's fine, really it is—which, in reality, only makes Lucy more annoyed.

Hard as it can be to do, leaving your partner alone precisely when you feel the strongest urge to pressure, pursue, and chase is sometimes the best option—a smart choice in terms of promoting not only your partner's sense of self-worth and well-being in the relationship but your own. When you can walk away from an ongoing, unresolved source of relationship stress, such as Chandra's chronic anger at Terry for not finishing the bathroom, chances are that you and your partner will find the contentment in your marriage increasing dramatically, because you've demonstrated to yourself *and* to him that you are not dependent on him to make you feel good about yourself, that you can thrive in a world without resolutions, and that you can operate independently to accomplish the things that are important to you. There is simply no overstating what a profound stress-relieving effect your letting go of these nagging and often unrealistic expectations and demands will have on your marriage. The other message you communicate to your partner when you drop these lost causes is: "*Our* happiness is more important than the bathroom. I can find another way. If something takes us down, it won't be something as dumb as this."

As discussed earlier in this book, sometimes in marriage the wisest course of action is: "Don't just *do* something. *Stand* there."

Not working on your relationship, *not* pouncing on problems and pressuring your partner to change signals to him that you have reached a point where the imperfections in you and your mate and your marriage don't obscure the pleasures. The relationship police have retired. You give him the marriage-transforming gift of allowing him room to breathe, think, and, possibly—not necessarily, but possibly—change of his own accord. You clear a space for something new and different to happen in its own time.

What all of this boils down to is: You don't always need your partner's participation, cooperation, or approval to change the dynamic in your relationship for the better. You can accomplish some part of that goal—perhaps more than you imagine—by changing your own attitudes and behavior.

What All Dedicated Do-It-Yourselfers Know:

Sometimes You Just Need to Get Out of the House

This is a good time to ask yourself when it was that you last giggled out loud without your husband or children around. Think about what you were doing and whom you were with. What does it tell you about people and activities you enjoy? Have you seen those folks or enjoyed those activities lately? If not, might it be time—perhaps past time—that you did? When's the last time you went somewhere, did something, or met someone new without your husband or children there with you? When's the last time you wanted to go somewhere or do something (see a movie, catch a special exhibit) but couldn't get one of them to join you so you didn't go? If it's been a while since you've given *yourself* some breathing room, I invite you to do the following:

1. Name three new things you'd like to do this month on your own.
2. Consider the fact that, if your husband and kids don't share a particular interest of yours, you will probably have a much better time if you *do* go alone. Say you want to see the Edward Hopper exhibit at the museum. Imagine being able to stand and stare at *Nighthawks* to your heart's content without your spouse or kids trying to hurry you along.
3. Now, pick one of these three things you'd like to do and go do it. See how it feels. See how you feel about yourself and your husband and family afterward. It may feel a bit uncomfortable at first if you aren't used to it, but it's important eventually to figure out how to enjoy giving yourself a little solo time.

Some possible activities:

• **Find new places to laugh and play.** Group affiliations of almost any kind will put more life in your life: from enrolling in a class on comedy writing to joining a book club, from taking up scuba diving to learning French. As tired as this advice seems, the reason you hear it over and over again is: It works. Without laughter and play, we can't thrive.

• **Disappear for a while.** Try the experiment called "a few days without him." Sometimes unhappiness comes from long-ignored, unmet needs for wildness and a little adventure. Spouses can make the mistake of expecting their partner and/or their relationship to always fulfill these needs. If that doesn't seem to be working (and it often doesn't), why not actively seek out adventure for yourself? Go off into the wild, whatever that may mean for you. Try a vision quest. Trek the Rockies. Descend the Grand Canyon. Visit your old roommate. After all, how can he miss you if you don't go away?

• **Ask yourself "What would Eleanor do?"** The late, great Eleanor Roosevelt once said, "Do one thing every day that scares you." She also said, "Yesterday is history, tomorrow is a mystery, today is a gift." This magnificent woman lived every day of her life to its fullest. She may not have had the happiest marriage, but she had more important things to do than sulk or feel sorry for herself. She was too busy holding press conferences, giving lectures, making radio broadcasts, and writing newspaper columns. She was too busy defying segregation by sitting among blacks and whites at a conference for human welfare in Birmingham, Alabama, in 1939 and opening the Army Nurse Corps to black women and joining the NAACP in 1945. She was too busy being elected head of the United Nations Human Rights Commission in 1946. What about you? What do you have to give that the world needs? There are lots of causes. Join a mentoring program. Volunteer at a soup kitchen. Deliver meals to the home-bound elderly. Run for political office. Help build an orphanage in Belize. Then come home and see if you can even remember what it was you were complaining about before you left. Instead of asking how life is treating you today, ask yourself: How are you treating life?

Remember, He Is *Your* Old Spouse

Anyone who has ever gone house hunting has stories to tell of real estate ads that didn't *quite* describe a house accurately: the "charming" house that turned out to be tiny; the "convenient loca-tion" that turned out to be on a highway across from a mall; the "pre-war" building that turned out to be pre–Civil War. As I men-tioned in Chapter 1, most house-hunters walk through dozens of homes they could never imagine living in before they find the one they want. *Live here?* they may think to themselves about the homes they reject. *I could never live here!*

Perhaps not. But someone else could. Usually, someone else has. In pretty much every case, unless a house is brand-new, some other person or family has already lived in this completely unacceptable house—and most likely not only lived in it but loved it, cared about it, maintained it, and filled it with laughter and life. And unless the house is being torn down, chances are that someone else will live in and love it again. Hard to believe, sometimes, but true.

In marriage as in home ownership, beauty is in the eye of the beholder. No house or marriage is perfect. Every home and every spouse and relationship has strengths and weaknesses, beauty and flaws. It doesn't matter if you couldn't imagine being married to someone else's husband. It doesn't matter if other women couldn't imagine being married to yours. He's not *their* old spouse. He's *your* old spouse. You chose him for a reason, and you've stayed with him for a reason. Not because he's perfect or because your relationship is perfect, but because, for all the quirks, tensions, imperfections, and problems in your marriage, this man and this relationship are right for you. Not perfect. But plenty good enough. A good fit.

When two people have a good-fit marriage, their relationship feels like the safest place in the world for both of them. That is a marriage worth working to enhance and preserve. If you've stuck with me this far, you've already done a tremendous amount of that work. So let me leave you with some thoughts on loving ways to maintain your relationship with your old spouse for the rest of your lives.

1. Love includes hate. As I pointed out in Chapter 3, a long-term marriage almost always involves falling in and out of and back in love with the same person over and over again. Bad times will come. When they do, try to say calm, embrace everything you're feeling, and remind yourself: "This too shall pass." Years ago, a marriage counselor I know told me that when his wife was upset with him about something, she would calmly announce, "I'm in hate with you today"—sometimes as soon as they rolled out of bed. Because she made this remark so calmly and even lovingly, he said, he didn't get defensive and put his guard up. He stayed open, they both stayed affectionate, and they talked. "Uh-oh," he'd say, joking but serious. "Okay, why are you in hate with me today?" She'd tell him, he'd listen, sometimes he'd respond immediately, sometimes he wouldn't. But the fact that they could have these exchanges so calmly almost always meant they were able to resolve the issue by that night.

2. Closeness includes distance. In a series of essays published in 1892, the philosopher Arthur Schopenhauer wrote a parable about a group of porcupines that tried to huddle together for warmth on a cold winter day. Every time they got close enough to start feeling warmer, they began pricking each other with their quills and had to move apart. But when they moved apart, they'd become cold and waddle back closer together. Back and forth, back and forth they went, trying to find the right balance between closeness and distance. Love works that way, too. Partners jockey to feel loved but not smothered, separate but not alone, connected but not entangled, independent but not apart. In some ways, this is how spouses live their entire lives together: coming closer, stepping back; drawing together, pulling away. As your relationship continues to evolve, stay flexible enough to change course, to tinker, to keep trying to find the right feeling in a particular moment (or month or year), even if what it takes to feel good keeps changing.

3. Attempt less, accomplish more. I mentioned in Chapter 1 that I always like to start my work with couples where *they* want to start—by addressing the problem that brought them to my office and working with the most easily fixable part of that problem first, to give spouses a sense of accomplishment, encouragement, and hope. I advise the couples I counsel to adopt this same approach when working on marital issues on their own—little by little, step by step, easy steps first. There's no rush. Remember, your marriage is a lifelong project.

4. You do your jobs, he does his. It may not always seem to you that your partner is carrying his fair share of the load in your marriage. And sometimes, in the short run, he may not be. But that doesn't mean that in the long run what he *does* do and *does* contribute isn't still essential—just as essential as your contributions, even though yours may seem (and may be) more numerous and obvious. Consider the following: Researchers in South Africa recently discovered that African mole rats don't share the work of maintaining their colony equally. In one study, it was found that 65 percent of the mole rats in a colony do about 95 percent of the daily work, while the other 35 percent laze around, mostly just eating. (Sound familiar?) The question: Why did the industrious mole rats put up with it? Why didn't they just kick the lazy mole rats out of the colony? The researchers learned the answer after a rain soaked the ground. Mole rats live underground. Everything they do, they do in tunnels. But they can't dig these tunnels when the earth is dry and hard—only when it's wet and soft. As soon as the rains softened the ground, suddenly the seemingly lazy mole rats sprang to action. Time to start digging! Time to expand the colony! Time to meet and mate with other colonies! Time to start new colonies of their own! The fat mole rats weren't merely being lazy. They were building up their strength and energy for the Big Boys' job of ensuring the mole rats' future. Husbands can be like that, too. They sit around, they eat, they don't do much around the house. But when you need one, aren't you glad you have one? Do you really want to be the one to change a tire during a winter snow storm or chase the raccoon out of the house? As one woman said to me about her twenty-eight-year marriage, "I'm still married because even when I can't stand him I can't imagine my life without him."

5. Love is full of miracles. After the devastating tsunami in Thailand, photos began to circulate on the Internet of a baby hippo that had lost its mother and, soon afterward, made a giant tortoise his surrogate family. This unlikely pair is shown walking, swimming, and sleeping together, with the hippo's head resting on the tortoise's shell or front leg.

It's an unforgettable lesson in adaptation, and it tugs at the heart of everyone who looks at the picture—not because it's about making the best out of what you've got, but because it shows that the deep need for love and connection transcends *everything*, especially our limited notions of who is capable of giving love to whom and what that bond is going to look like.

In the end, it is not who we love or how we love or even where we love that matters most to men, women, and the future of humankind.

It is *that* we love, despite all obstacles and fears. After reading this book, maybe you will throw a spousewarming party to honor your love and the work you and your husband have done to strengthen and deepen it. Perhaps you will invite only each other, or maybe you will share the night with a house full of friends and celebrate your love that way. Or both. Because, after all your hard work, you are now getting a wonderful return on your investment. A celebration is in order.

For all the years we hang in there, for all the disappointment and stress, and for all the masterpiece moments of falling in love with the same person all over again, I turn to novelist Amy Bloom, who said it best: "Love at first sight is easy to understand; it's when two people have been looking at each other for a lifetime that it becomes a miracle."

As you continue with your renovations, work as if the deepest happiness you will ever know in life depends on it. When you begin to lose faith or lose heart, pull out your blueprint and remember the wonder of what you're trying to create. Take another look at that hammer. You aren't pounding away at nothing. You're building a life together with all the richness that life can hold.

Appendix

FEMA for Relationships: Federal Emergency Marital Aid

When and Where to Seek Professional Help

Disasters happen. Sometimes we see them coming. Sometimes we don't. Even when we do, we can be or feel helpless in the face of them. If you've turned to this appendix first because your marriage feels like a disaster and none of the preceding chapters seem to speak to you at this time, take a deep breath. You may be right about the state of your marriage, but you may be wrong. There is no easy way for me to help you make that determination only from what I've written in this book. I urge you instead to consider seeking professional help and guidance in making that determination for yourself. In this section, I will help you find the help you may want or need—with or without your partner.

First Things First! You Need *Immediate* Help If:

- You feel that you or your children are unsafe in your relationship.

- You or your partner has been physically abusive with the other or the children.
- You or your partner is physically or verbally threatening toward the other or the children.
- You or your partner is obsessively jealous or possessive.
- You or your partner abuses alcohol or drugs.

Contact the following organizations for help:

- National Coalition Against Domestic Violence
  www.ncadv.org
- The National Domestic Violence Hotline
  www.ndvh.org
  1-800-799-SAFE (1-800-799-7233); 800-787-3224 (TTY)
- Al-Anon/Alateen
  www.al-anon.org
  888-4AL-ANON (888-425-2666)
- Phoenix House
  www.phoenixhouse.org

You may also need or want professional help if:

- Your health is suffering because of the relationship.
- Your children are being negatively affected by your marital problems and/or your parenting abilities have suffered because of these problems.
- You or your partner is severely depressed or unhappy and has been for more than thirty days.
- You or your partner has been unfaithful or feels a strong urge to be unfaithful.

- A friend, relative, or other third party is overly intrusive in your relationship.
- You are aware of serious problems in the relationship but don't know how to deal with them, and they are only getting worse.
- You and your partner are both trying to make things better between you, but you aren't seeing any improvements.

Where to Get Good Help

The best way to find a therapist is to ask friends or family members for a referral. When people are helped through therapy they are often happy to pass along the name of the professional they worked with, in the sincere hope that others can be helped, too. You don't have to disclose any private information when you ask friends or relatives for a referral. You can simply say that you are looking for someone but would prefer not to discuss why. If a friend or relative does recommend someone to you, ask the person who is making the recommendation:

- Why did you like this therapist?
- How long did you see/have you been seeing this therapist?
- What can you tell me about how this therapist likes to work?
- Would you mind telling me how much this therapist charges?

If you're not comfortable asking someone you know for a recommendation, you can also find a good therapist in your area by contacting:

- The American Association for Marriage and Family Therapy www.aamft.org

- National Association of Social Workers
  www.socialworkers.org
  800-638-8799
- American Association of Sexuality Educators Counselors
  and Therapists
  www.aasect.org
  804-752-0026

If you can't afford the costs of regular therapy (usually $100 or more, sometimes much more, per 50-minute hour), you might want to contact hospitals, health clinics, colleges and universities, and training institutions in your area to see whether they offer low-cost services. Some hospitals have low-cost outpatient health clinics, for example. Some medical, psychiatric, and psychotherapeutic training institutions also offer free or low-cost services in exchange for clients agreeing to be observed by or have their sessions videotaped for students in training. If you don't mind agreeing to this, you can often get very good treatment at a reasonable price. One couple I know who decided to go this route (they agreed to participate in a therapeutic pilot study) received treatment from two of the most respected couples therapists practicing today—for peanuts! You can usually find training institutions in your area by looking in the Yellow Pages under "psychotherapy," "mental health," or "social service agencies."

Picking Up the Phone

When you call a therapist who has been recommended to you, say, "Lisa and Tom Jones gave me your name" or "I got your name from the AAMFT website." Then say, "My fiancé/husband/partner and I are interested in therapy. Do you have a moment to talk?" Then:

• Briefly describe the main problem you and your partner are seeking help for and ask the therapist if she has experience in this area.

• Briefly ask the therapist to tell you about his background: Is he licensed? How long has he been in practice? Is he specially trained in couples and/or family therapy? This last point is important. Someone who might be a superb individual therapist may not necessarily be a good couples counselor. These are two different specialties that require different training and skills.

• Ask if the therapist is accepting new patients and whether she could accommodate the schedule that works best for you and your partner.

• Ask the therapist's fee. Ask if he accepts your insurance. Ask if she will see clients on a sliding scale (lower fees for people who can't afford the usual fee). If the therapist came very highly recommended, does not offer sliding fees, and the full fee is high but not outrageously high, I'd urge you to seriously consider entering therapy with this professional. You don't always get what you pay for (many people have horror stories to tell about bad therapy), but you often do. And paying a good therapist a little more could actually end up being more economical than paying a less-experienced therapist a lower fee, depending on how long you remain in therapy. In the right hands, couples may begin seeing improvements in their relationship within three to five sessions. If a therapist's fee really is

out of the ballpark, ask if he or she can refer you to someone you can
more easily afford.

The Initial Visit

During a first session, try to get a sense of:

• **The therapist's agenda**. A good therapist won't have a personal
or professional investment in helping you and your partner stay
together *or* part ways. Ultimately, that's up to the two of you. The
therapist's primary task is to help the two of you decide what *you*
want. If you want to stay together, the therapist will try to help you
do that in ways that are healthy for you both.

• **The therapist's neutrality**. Does the therapist make both of you
feel comfortable, listened to, and respected? You might be drawn to
a therapist who seems to be "on your side," but beware of one who
is. Any therapist who takes sides cannot help you and your partner
develop the crucial ability to think and act in threes: what's good for
you, what's good for him, and what's good for the relationship. Both
partners must feel understood and validated in order for growth
and healing to occur. If it doesn't feel like that is happening, ask
about it because sometimes you may feel the therapist is taking sides
when, in reality, he or she isn't.

• **Conflicts of interest**. A therapist can treat a couple as a couple,
or she can counsel *one or the other* partner individually. She *cannot*
treat a couple as a couple *and* treat one partner individually. And a
therapist certainly cannot treat a couple as a couple *and both partners*

individually. Too many complications arise when secrets are shared in individual sessions and remain unspoken in couple sessions. A reputable couples therapist may want to see partners separately for a session or two, to get a better sense of them as individuals in order to better help them as a couple—but that's all. In fact, I'd advise you to quit ongoing counseling *of any kind* with a therapist who offers to counsel either one of you individually at the same time that he is also willing to treat you as a couple. Find a new couples therapist, and if either or both of you should decide you could benefit from individual treatment as well, ask this therapist to recommend someone else—one for you, and one for your partner.

• **Who sets the therapeutic goals.** Many therapists need a few sessions to get to know new clients and understand their backgrounds—the kinds of relationships you were exposed to as you grew up, the kinds of stressors that exist in your family of origin. But if the therapist seems primarily interested in probing your pasts whereas you primarily want to work on a real-time, present-day issue or problem, speak up. A good therapist may need to continue probing your backgrounds here and there during sessions to help you resolve a present-day problem, but you want to know that the therapist is willing to follow your lead and concentrate on the goals you set for yourself.

Going It Alone

As I pointed out in Chapter 11, you don't always need your partner's participation, cooperation, or approval to change the dynamic in your relationship for the better. You can accomplish some part of that goal—perhaps more than you imagine—simply by changing your own attitudes and behavior. Therapy can absolutely help you do that, whether your partner chooses to enter therapy with you or not. If your partner decides "no" and you decide "yes," you have a choice between entering individual therapy or group therapy. Both can be incredibly valuable. Each has its strengths.

Group Therapy

If you mainly want to work on relationship and social problems—that is, if you mostly want to learn better ways of asserting your own needs in all your relationships, for example, or how to be generally more receptive, respectful, and sensitive to other people's feelings and needs, group therapy is the way to go. A group, like a marriage, is a "feeling gym" that challenges you to examine your own actions and reactions toward an assortment of people in a range of emotionally challenging and charged situations. It's a real eye-opener and skill-builder. Group therapy teaches you how to speak your mind forthrightly yet kindly, and how to give and receive respectful, constructive feedback. To find a group in your area (if you cannot get a recommendation from someone you know), contact the American Group Psychotherapy Association (www.agpa.org), which offers information about groups and referrals. Another advantage of group: It usually costs less.

Individual Therapy

If your relationship has serious problems, and your partner refuses to admit to or work on these problems, and you feel unable to take any action; if you know you shouldn't act or react the way you do but you can't seem to help it; or if you know you should stand up for and set limits for yourself but you can't seem to do it, individual therapy may be your best choice. Some indications that it may be right for you:

• You are certain your partner has lied to you, or he gets inappropriately angry or pushy, but instead of naming and discussing the problem, you pretend it didn't happen. Or you blow up inappropriately, or initiate or acquiesce to "makeup" sex and tell yourself that this fixes everything. Or you send him a love note or tell him how much you love him to make everything all right, or you apologize and take the blame to smooth things over.

• You tell yourself that whatever problems your relationship may have, once you have a baby, or once the baby gets older, or once your partner gets a better job, or once you get a job, or once you quit and stay home full-time—and so on—things will improve.

If you identify with so much as one part of the above statements, I urge you to find a counselor who can help you examine and alter the beliefs and behaviors that are keeping you trapped and unhappy. Again, the sources to obtain referrals to couples counselors listed in this appendix can also help you find someone to see individually. You owe it to yourself to do it, whether you believe it or not. You deserve a long and happy life and a long and happy marriage: perhaps with your current partner (there's no telling how things might improve when you take independent steps to change the dynamic between you); perhaps not. The only way to give your current relationship the best possible chance for success is for one of you, at least, to seek professional counseling. If your partner won't do it, then you must. If you change for the better and he really loves you and wants the relationship to work as much as you do, he may be inspired to work on himself and change for the better, too. If he doesn't, if he won't, if he can't, then you will always know that you did everything you could to salvage the relationship.

AKNOWLEDGMENTS

To Charles Salzberg and Ross Klavan, who told me to write this book—thanks so much for insisting. I am grateful for the support of Philip Dacey, who kept me laughing and thinking. Thanks to the Levine Greenberg Agency, Monika Verma, and my agent, Stephanie Rostan, who was a gentle and tough shepherd through this process. Thanks to Laureen Rowland and Danielle Friedman, my smart editors, and Marie Coolman and Liz Keenan in publicity, for their commitment and expertise along the way—especially Danielle for that last late-night push. Thanks to Jaci Powers for all her help. Thanks to John Morrone for copyediting this manuscript so carefully. I have many friends who helped me through this year and a half: David Sparr, John Pinto, Lynn Kwalwassar, Michelle Wolf, Debra Wolf, Ian Mackler, Norma and Milton Rubin, Karen Armstrong, the Katharine Butler gallery, and Tom Wolbarst. A special thanks to Jen Greenberg for her photo, to Daniel Perlman for the website, and to Bob Adamo for saving my hard drive. Many thanks to my clients who have shared their stories through the years.

They are all unrecognizable here. I have tried to keep the heart of their stories while the details have all been changed. They are my teachers. I've saved two special people for last. The first is Gini Kopecky Wallace for her enthusiasm, commitment, and sharp writing skills—I could not have done this without her. And I thank my late friend Betsy Carpenter, who read drafts until the very end. Betsy, I will miss you more than words can say.